The Compelling Speaker

How to Transform Your Voice
for Maximum Impact,
Persuasion, and Connection

John Henny

JHVS Virtual, LLC
4343 MacArthur Blvd. #1073
Newport Beach, CA 92660
www.johnhenny.com

Although the author and publisher have made every effort to ensure that the information in this book was correct at press time, the author and publisher do not assume and hereby disclaim any liability to any party for any loss, damage, or disruption caused by errors or omissions, whether such errors or omissions result from negligence, accident, or any other cause.

The publisher and the author strongly recommend you consult with your ear, nose, and throat doctor (ENT) before beginning any voice program. The author is not a licensed healthcare care provider and represents that they have no expertise in diagnosing, examining, or treating vocal medical conditions of any kind, or in determining the effect of any specific exercise on a medical condition.

You should understand when participating in any vocal exercises, there is the possibility of physical injury. If you engage in these vocal exercises, you agree that you do so at your own risk, are voluntarily participating in these activities, assume all risk of injury to yourself, and agree to release and discharge the publisher and the author from any and all claims or causes of action, known or unknown, arising out of the contents of this book.

The publisher and the author advise you to take full responsibility for your safety and know your limits. Before practicing the skills described in this book, be sure that your voice is healthy enough for exercising and do not take risks beyond your level of experience, aptitude, training, and comfort level.

Get Your Free Bonus Materials

Welcome to The Compelling Speaker!

PLEASE NOTE:

I have created online videos to assist you in studying this material.

There will be points in the book where I will prompt you to find a supplemental online lesson in your book members' area.

Please go to CompellingSpeakerBook.com to access your free bonus content.

Contents

CHAPTER ONE

Your Hidden Asset

"The world is waiting for your words."
– ARVEE ROBINSON

W hat is the voice? This question can bring up a host of different answers:

It is our primary means of communication and emotional connection.

It is an instrument so complex that voice scientists are still working to unlock its mysteries.

It is the means to obtain many of our goals and desires.

It is human flesh that can be damaged or destroyed.

And yet so few of us give the voice much thought until we temporarily have issues due to illness or abuse or begin to lose it completely.

My goal is to change your relationship with your voice and illustrate how it can be one of your greatest assets in business and life. I will also give you techniques to help it last a lifetime.

I've been a voice teacher and coach for over 30 years. I've worked with superstar singers and elite performers. Yet, singing did not come naturally to me. It was (and occasionally still is) a struggle, but this struggle has allowed me to experience many of the issues others experience with their voice. And this journey enables me to find and fix vocal issues quickly.

In my early work with singers, I was occasionally asked to work with non-singing voice professionals such as actors, announcers and executives. I discovered that the principles of singing are equally applicable to speech. These fundamental components, when appropriately utilized, can turn a mediocre or uninspiring speaker into a charismatic and engaging communicator.

And the good news is these transformations can happen in a relatively short period of time. While singers need to build and navigate the extreme limits of the voice, speakers work within a much smaller framework, yet the building and improvement of this area will yield dramatic results.

Imagine having a voice that others enjoy listening to. The confidence from being able to capture and hold attention. The ability to effectively communicate and persuade with energy and emotional connection.

How would this voice affect your career, your earnings, your relationships?

Would this voice change how you feel when asked to give a presentation or those moments just before you walk on stage to give a public talk?

"But I have a terrible voice," you say.

I say you are wrong.

Every voice, unless hampered by physical damage or neurological issues, is capable of sounding fantastic. And even a damaged voice can be greatly improved. It takes awareness, some knowledge, and a bit of work.

I can give you the awareness and knowledge; all you need to do is take a few minutes each day to employ what I will show you. These concepts and exercises work. I have taught thousands of students, and the voice teachers I have trained, work with tens of thousands more. Some of these voice users are household names. Others are doing superstar work in their professions and daily lives.

You don't need to have the genetic vocal gifts of a Beyoncé or Morgan Freeman; you only need to sound like you - the BEST version of you. This is what will authentically connect you with your listener.

I look forward to hearing your best voice.

CHAPTER TWO

Using This Book

W hile it is tempting to say this book is for everyone, I have focused on a certain level of professional voice users.

If your voice and ability to effectively communicate are central to your career and livelihood, this book is for you. On a side note: if you already have a great sounding, expressive voice, I will show you how to keep it that way.

Are you being listened to? I mean, heard in the way you intend.

Let me further ask:

Are your ideas, pitches, meetings, lectures, sales calls, and presentations getting the desired results? Are you commanding attention? Do you have the ability to regain attention when you feel it slip? Are you able to convince on a deep, emotional level? Are your inspiration and passion contagious? Can you reach others with your voice and inspire them?

If these questions speak to you, then this book is for you.

Your ideas, services, products, and leadership are important, even vital to the livelihoods of yourself and others, but if your voice is not connecting and commanding attention, you can be lost in the noise.

I want your voice heard, your inner music (yes, music) to be an irresistible song, your voice vibrating with emotional intention, melody, and rhythm.

The universe is vibration. The neurons in your brain respond to resonance and frequencies (the speed of vibration). Your voice is simply vibrating air molecules of varying rates of speed and energy, yet these vibrations are profound and directly impact your life and career.

My goals are not only to improve your voice but to inspire you to better communication. I want you to celebrate these incredibly complex vibrations and tune them for maximum connection and impact. I want you to realize the miracle of communication within you, this voice you are likely currently using (and possibly abusing) with little thought or awareness.

Let's celebrate your unique and wonderful voice!

I recommend first reading through this book once. I have kept the text on the lean side, focusing on the key areas of voice and the steps necessary to enhance your awareness, vocal technique, and health. I know you are busy and need to get a return on your time investment.

Once you have an understanding of the voice and how to improve it, I suggest working on the exercises for a few minutes each day. Consistency is more important than the length of a practice session. The goal is not only to strengthen and enhance your voice but also to increase your awareness of your voice. Awareness is your main lever for improvement as you go through your day.

I have created a bonus member's area for this book, featuring video examples of some of the exercises. You can find them at compellingspeakerbook.com.

Also, don't hesitate to contact me and my team at <u>frontdesk@compellingspeaker.com</u> with your comments and questions. We are here to help you find your most compelling voice.

CHAPTER THREE

Discovering My Voice

"There's nothing more powerful than the human voice."

– LEONTYNE PRICE

I was in choir, and I was miserable. As a third grader, the last thing I wanted to do was stand and sing - I wanted to be tearing around the playground playing football or tetherball (my particular favorite).

We were learning "Tie a Yellow Ribbon Round the Old Oak Tree," an early 1970s hit for Tony Orlando and Dawn. The song had a payoff line: "Now the whole damn bus is cheering." Since we were young children in a public school, our choir director had changed the offensive "damn" to "darn," and I was having none of it.

I stood there refusing to sing, occasionally mouthing the words but emitting no sound. Our harried director was, I'm sure, aware of my quiet rebellion, but she had 30 other children to worry about.

I kept up my pantomime act until the chosen moment...just as we came to our director's appropriately safe substitution, I yelled at the top of my lungs, "DAMN!"

So yes, you are reading a book by a vocal expert who was thrown out of choir.

My journey to the world of voice was a winding path that started with no intention of landing here.

As I became more interested in music, I would attempt to sing along with my favorite songs, but the results were less than satisfactory. I decided I was one of those who couldn't sing and took up the drums at age twelve. By my late teens, I was getting paid for my efforts.

In my early 20s, I had a roommate start vocal lessons with someone who studied with Stevie Wonder's teacher. That was good enough for me! That teacher, Eric Fütterer, showed me the mechanics of the voice that allowed me to gain levels of control I had never conceived of.

I figured I could get proficient enough to add backing vocals to my drumming, which could help me get more work. Little did I know my life would completely change.

After a few years, I not only started getting better, but within two years, I was a lead singer, no longer behind the drums. I also began studying directly with Stevie Wonder's teacher himself, Seth Riggs, a giant in the world of voice.

As my understanding of the voice grew, I started showing other vocalists how to solve vocal issues using the tools I had been taught. This soon turned into full-time teaching.

The next shift was discovering voice science and becoming fascinated with how this miraculous instrument worked.

Two bits of soft tissue, ligament, and muscle the size of your thumbnail that can be heard over an orchestra--the voice can create not only a myriad of sounds and textures but also carry language. No other instrument can match its wonders.

I kept delving into the voice and started working with higher-level singers, including session vocalists, Broadway performers, and even music-industry superstars.

I started being sought out not only by singers but also speakers who were struggling with their voices. One of the first was a very successful trial attorney in vocal crisis.

This attorney had been to other voice experts, but his situation was not improving. He was experiencing extreme vocal weakness and fatigue. His voice was so problematic that he started avoiding social situations where he might have to talk in louder environments. And, of course, he worried about the impact on his work and ability to advocate for his clients.

I listened to his voice and deep concerns and started working the same exercises and approaches I used for singers but modified to focus on the speaking range. Even though this person did not sing (and had no desire to do so), the exercises began to work and stretch the small ligaments and muscles of the voice as well as his breath control.

Within six weeks, his voice had changed entirely. He excitedly shared how he had gone to a quite noisy event, and everyone could hear him. People from his wife to coworkers heard and saw the transformation. The worried person who had first come to my studio was now brimming with confidence, standing taller and smiling.

He then showed his appreciation by writing me a check for ten times my rate! I realized I needed to work with more speakers!

I have since worked with professional voice users, from managers to executives, voiceover artists, stage and film actors, from famous magicians to the US military.

In my journey, I discovered the voice is core to who we are as humans and that what makes a great singer also makes a great speaker.

I am passionate about bringing these incredible techniques to professional voice users everywhere. I hope to ignite a passion for your voice and a new level of communication and connection with others.

CHAPTER FOUR

Your Hidden Power

*"The art of communication is the
language of leadership."*
– JAMES HUMES

WHAT IS YOUR VOICE COSTING YOU?

The word "cost" usually brings one word to the fore: money. And your voice is likely costing you some amount of it.

Think of all the activities and situations that bring you or your business cash flow. How many of them involve using your voice?

You must convince and persuade potential buyers and clients, build an audience, inspire sales teams, educate staff, and get your ideas implemented. Now, think of the possible results if you could improve these situations by just 10%.

Imagine if you could convince 10% more of your clients, be 10% more of an inspiration, or gain a 10% advantage in attention that pushes your ideas forward.

What would that mean for your income, your business, or your career?

In all these situations, we need one thing: listeners, and listening is not a passive event. People need to engage their attention to focus on you specifically. Your words need to help different regions of the brain become involved.

The difference in the brain activity of an engaged listener can be seen with MRI imaging. When you lose the listener's attention, the brain remains active, but in a different way. The default mode network (DMN) often takes over.

The DMN is activated during passive rest and mind-wandering, which often involves daydreaming, thinking about others, about oneself, remembering the past, and planning for the future.

If you do not keep the listener actively engaged, connected, and interested, nature has this mental escape hatch, and once the listener has taken it, your ability to be heard rapidly diminishes.

What happens when listening to someone compelling?

When speakers are engaging and charismatic, they stimulate multiple brain areas. For example, the prefrontal cortex, which is involved in attention, planning, and decision-making, is activated as the listener pays close attention.

The language-processing areas work to understand the speaker's words and interpret their meaning. The limbic system, involved in emotion, activates as the speaker's words evoke feelings. There is more empathy and understanding as the mirror neuron system is engaged. If the speaker uses vivid imagery or tells a story, the visual processing areas of the listener's brain light up. An engaging speaker also elicits stronger neural synchrony, or "brain-to-brain coupling," where the listener's brain activity aligns more closely with the speaker's voice.

The results are drastically different when the speaker fails to actively involve the listener. All these areas become less engaged as the DMN takes over. Listeners appear present, but they are likely ruminating about their next meeting, where to go for lunch, or how to slip away gracefully.

Success is about finding the edges, those small advantages that your competitors miss. The voice is a huge edge that most miss; they never even think about it. When you can deeply connect with a client, an employee, or an investor, you gain a considerable advantage.

Research shows that emotion plays a massive role in our decision making (even if we don't realize it). Persons with damage to the emotional processing area of the brain struggle with decision making even when their logic reasoning abilities remain intact. We cannot make decisions without emotional context.

As we will discover, the voice is our primary emotional connector and communicator. You can reclaim the professional advantages you previously missed by holding attention and eliciting an emotional response.

THE POWER OF YOUR VOICE

The ancient Greeks recognized the power of the voice over 1500 years ago. Rhetoric, the art of effective and persuasive speaking or writing, was considered an essential skill, with public speaking being particularly prized.

Great orators began to codify what made their talks compelling and persuasive. The Sophists were among the first to create a school around persuasive speech. They got such good results that controversy soon followed, as their persuasive vocal techniques allowed poor reasoning to triumph over the pursuit of truth.

The great orator traditions spread to Rome, where the "modes of delivery" were developed, which took note of how great speakers controlled aspects of their voice for maximum effect.

The modes included volume, pitch, pace, and tone--the same devices great singers use.

The study of the voice's influence continues today, with researchers recently comparing millions of spoken samples and input from thousands of recruiters and consumers. From this data they have developed technology that can listen to a voice and determine how it will make the average listener feel. The accuracy rate is currently 75%, which is quite impressive for a bit of tech.

We often hear that 55% percent of communication is non-verbal, and it is true that raising an eyebrow or a shrug of the shoulders can influence the meaning of what is being said. However, researchers at Yale University decided to look closer at the role of the voice, particularly in the communication of emotion.

Researchers took over 1,700 participants through a series of exercises with the goal of accurately understanding what the other person was feeling emotionally. In one test, the subjects could see and hear each other. In another, they could only see body language, no sound. Finally, the researchers removed the visual element by turning out the lights or placing a divider between the subjects.

The results showed conclusively that empathetic accuracy improved when only hearing the voice and that body language distracted us from the core and truth of the speaker's feelings.

Effective emotional connection and communication leads to better workplace conflict resolution, improved personal relationships, and the ability to navigate complex social and political networks. In addition, I have found the more clients work on their voice awareness and abilities, the more their perception of what others are feeling and communicating is improved.

If there is one edge your competitors are likely missing, it is in harnessing the power of the voice, emotional connection, and empathy.

I imagine you are like a number of my clients--this is the first time you've genuinely thought about the consequences of ignoring your speaking voice and its effect on others.

I want to get you excited about this miracle of an instrument you house within your body, to understand its power, and to harness the incredible benefits of a great sounding and emotionally driven voice.

You will no longer struggle to be heard (both literally and figuratively). Instead, you will know how to capture and hold attention and make the dullest, driest material more interesting and engaging.

I will show you how to find your best voice and tap into the natural music hidden within.

I will guide you through the key techniques that singers use to keep an audience spellbound and how to apply them to your speaking voice.

While this is not a book about singing, the side benefit from all this is that your singing voice will improve (or you may discover you actually can sing). The bottom line is I will show you how to use your voice to keep your audience engaged.

In the next chapter, we will look at common issues with the speaking voice and how you can increase your awareness to improve your communication skills.

CHAPTER FIVE

Common Speaking Issues

"The human voice is the organ of the soul."
– HENRY WADSWORTH LONGFELLOW

T he voice is a complex instrument, and like any finely tuned machine, it can experience technical issues that diminish its effectiveness. In this chapter, I will address a few of the most common technique issues I find with speaking voices. Keep a measure of self-awareness and honesty to see if any of these apply to you.

PITCH

Your voice has a natural pitch range that is optimal for your unique instrument, and this range has a general center. The center is known as "optimal speaking pitch" (OSP). Not centering the voice on your OSP is often mistake number one.

We tend to associate deeper, richer voices with authority and confidence, and there is truth in this assumption. However, as in most things, humans take things too far. Often what we hear in a commanding voice is not so much lower pitch but rather better resonance, which brings out the fullness of the sound waves, including the warm lower frequencies. Resonance is essential to a great sounding voice, which we will look at shortly.

When trying to create (consciously or, usually, unconsciously) a more authoritative voice, the pitch often drops below our OSP. This results in a loss of acoustic energy (more on this later). This energy loss results in lower output or volume, making it harder for others to hear you.

The voice can increase in amplitude or loudness in two primary ways: more resistance at your vocal cords or an increase in acoustic energy. Lower pitches vibrate slower than higher ones, and if not reinforced with acoustic resonance energy, they are often harder to hear, especially in noisy environments.

We've all experienced being in a busy restaurant with someone who speaks with a low, dull voice. The ambient background sounds crowd out the lower frequency spectrum. In these situations, our ears need higher frequency elements in the voice that lift above the din and allow us to discern what is being said. Absent this higher acoustic energy, the speaker's voice is lost to the surrounding noise. These situations result in a lot of head nodding with no clue as to what you are politely agreeing to.

If the speaker picks up on the fact they are not being heard, they usually increase the volume not by raising the pitch or improving their resonance. They instead press the vocal cords together with more muscle.

Note: the correct term for "vocal cords" is "vocal folds" or simply "folds." I will refer to the vocal cords as vocal folds or folds going forward.

By pressing the folds with more intensity, they do get a bit louder, but in an incredibly inefficient way. As a result, the voice continues to lack the high-frequency energy that the ear seeks. Also, this excessive pressing can cause the folds to fatigue and swell, leading to hoarseness and even a loss of the voice. Over time, this overuse can cause chronic vocal issues requiring therapy, extended periods of vocal rest (complete silence), and even surgery.

When we find and use our OSP, the voice can be heard in large rooms and noisy environments. You will also be able to speak for more extended periods without debilitating vocal fatigue. I will show you how to find and maintain your OSP in this book.

BREATHINESS

Breathiness is the opposite of over-pressing the voice. As we will see in the next chapter, the voice is incredibly complex, yet it breaks down into three main elements, one of these being the resistance of airflow at the vocal folds.

The vocal folds work much like a trumpet player's lips, quickly opening and closing to create the sound waves we turn into speech. If the folds do not fully close or resist the upcoming air for the right amount of time, we get a relatively weak sound wave. This weakness can be heard as a very soft or light voice, all the way to excessive breathiness. This type of voice production is not only harder to hear, but it can also fatigue the speaker. Feelings of running out of breath or irritation at the folds from the excess air can lead to vocal issues.

RANGE

Range is related to pitch but refers to the variety of pitches we use. While we have an OSP, we don't want to be stuck there. A wider range of pitches will give your voice a sense of melody and is more expressive of emotion and intent. On the other hand, if we speak on a monotone, or if our pitch sequence is predictable (think of listening to "Three Blind Mice" on repeat), the listener will likely tune you out.

TONE

Tone distinguishes your voice and makes you sound like "you." Contrary to what some believe, tone is not set in stone; you have a broad palette of potential tonal colors. A great impressionist can sound exactly like someone else, but they do this with their unique vocal equipment. When they are not in character, impressionists sound like themselves. Such is the capacity we have to change what we sound like.

While we all have a broad tonal palette, there is a natural tonal spectrum for each of us. Finding and nurturing your genuine and unique tone colors will bring out your best and most trustworthy voice.

If you don't like the sound of your voice and are worried others share your opinion, rest assured you can quickly change and improve your tone.

EMOTIONAL INTENTION

The issue I believe costs speakers more than almost any other is the lack of emotion and intention. Its relevance extends not only to impassioned circumstances, but also to routine exchanges.

The word "emotion" brings thoughts of laughter, anger, or tears, but emotion driven by specific intent is an essential tool in so many professional situations (and it works in your personal life as well).

A team leader is about to give a presentation on a new budget and earnings expectations. As they take their seats, team members experience emotions ranging from curiosity and excitement to anxiety and resistance.

Suppose this presentation is given as a flat, non-intentioned recitation of numbers, projections, and goals. In that case, the positive emotions will likely subside, and anyone feeling negative emotions may leave the meeting worse off.

But how can numbers and projections have emotion? By setting firm and clear emotional intentions before the meeting starts. Instead of forcing yourself to be enthusiastic or motivated, you choose to inform or inspire.

By focusing on intentions, you will naturally have more energy and emotion in your voice. In addition, since the voice is the primary communicator of emotion, your words will land differently.

Every team member in that room is wired from birth to discern emotion and truth from the vibrations of the voice (this is why those who abuse speaking skills are very dangerous indeed. I have never seen a cult leader or con artist with a poor-sounding, emotionally disconnected voice).

The energy of your intentions can change everything from interviews and sales calls to explaining how software works.

I will show you how to utilize this powerful skill later in this book.

Now let's discuss why you may not like the current sound of your voice.

CHAPTER SIX

Embracing Your Voice

"Your uniqueness is your strength. Remember:
you are an original voice. Cherish it."
— BRIAN RATHBONE

Y ou walk out the door feeling fantastic.

Everything came together in just the right way, and you know your outfit looks great. There is an extra boost of confidence as you arrive at your destination and begin to greet people with a sparkle in your eye.

Then...disaster. Someone (or, in my case, usually me) spills a horribly colored substance on your clothes. Now that confidence is instantly gone, replaced by thoughts of "how do I cover this up" or "do I need to leave?"

Feeling good about yourself makes a huge difference, and your voice, though you may not have thought about it in this way, is the same.

Imagine feeling great about the sound of your voice and knowing others enjoy listening to you. How much of a difference would that make in your life and career?

But many of us think the same thing when we hear a recording of ourselves: "is that what I sound like?!"

Depending on the quality of the recording, the answer ranges from mostly to absolutely.

Why does our voice sound so different, and why do we usually dislike it?

Does my voice sound different to me than it does to others? In a word, yes.

There are several reasons for this, but primarily when you speak, your voice travels away from you and toward others. Sound waves are like waves in the ocean. The waves in the air are caused by air molecules becoming excited by your vocal folds and vocal tract (your throat and mouth). These vibrating molecules bump into neighboring molecules, which bump into the next neighbors, all the way to the listener's ears.

While you are the engine that starts the vibrations, this energy is not for you but for your intended listener. The energy hits their ears in a more focused way as the wave is pointed at them. Your experience of your voice is closer to listening to someone who is facing away from you. It's harder to hear.

Nature makes up for this by conducting a certain amount of sound through bone. Bone conduction occurs when sound vibrations travel through the bones of your skull and reach your inner ear, bypassing the traditional pathway of sound entering through the outer ear. This results in a different perception of your voice compared to how it sounds when heard through the air.

The bone-conducted sound has a distinct quality, often described as deeper and more resonant than how your voice sounds when heard through the air. This is because bone conduction emphasizes lower frequencies, which can give your voice a richer and fuller tone.

I will show you how to increase the richness and fullness of your voice so you sound great to others, not just to yourself.

One of the main themes of this book is to not only become more aware of your voice, but to fall in love with this miracle instrument. I want you to love the sound of your voice.

Your voice is your acoustic identity, and exclusively yours. Embrace your voice and celebrate its sonic uniqueness. By doing the exercises in this book, you won't so much change your voice as unveil its full potential and beauty.

The vibrations of your voice not only connect you with others but also with yourself. Most religions and spiritual practices incorporate some form of voice work, from singing to chanting.

For the speaker, the vibrations of their voice can have a positive psychological impact. The way their voice resonates within the body can create a sense of self-awareness and personal connection to the emotions they are expressing. This can influence our emotional state, confidence, and overall well-being.

INCREASING AWARENESS

The fact that you are reading these words puts you far ahead of most voice users. You have chosen to increase your awareness of the voice and its vital role in your life.

Let's explore further awareness of the voice with a series of questions:

- How does your voice generally feel in the morning? Does it take some time to get going?

- Does your voice get tired or even hoarse during a long day?
- Does your voice ever feel weak and lacking energy?
- Are you often clearing your throat? If unsure, ask someone close to you (this is often done without being aware).
- Is thick, excess phlegm, or mucous in your voice an issue?
- Do you feel as if you run out of breath when speaking?
- Do others often ask you to repeat yourself?
- Do you feel you are not being listened to or have difficulty holding the other person's attention?
- Are you often interrupted?
- When presenting or speaking in front of a group are you calm and present, or is your mind racing elsewhere?

As you go about your day, keep an open awareness about your voice, your connection to it, and how it affects others. This is not an exercise of self-criticism but merely a stocktaking of your current vocal situation.

One of the first things I do when working with a client is to get a clear picture of the current state of their voice, both through discussing their current voice use as well as listening to and doing small tests.

Once we have this clear understanding, we can start making fast, effective changes.

Some of the issues you will find with your voice are technical; others are issues of vocal health and lifestyle, and some result from mindset.

I will address all the significant challenges I find in speakers and give you steps to take control of your voice. Some of these may connect with you, and some may not. However, I advise going through all the challenges and exercises at least once because issues can come and go in our speaking voice, and I want you to have the tools to keep your voice in top shape at all times.

THE WORK AHEAD

Although we will use exercises I often employ with my singing clients, you don't have to worry if you think you can't sing. I argue almost everyone can sing, but that's another discussion for another day. I will say that if you practice these exercises, a side benefit is that your singing voice will improve.

This book will improve your voice in a number of ways, from building strength and agility to increasing the quality of tone and resonance. This will give you a much more expressive instrument.

We will also focus on best health practices and warm-ups to keep your voice in top shape throughout your life.

A portion of the book is dedicated to bringing music into your speech. Again, this is an incredibly powerful approach that will give you the ability to hold interest and the confidence in knowing you are being listened to.

Finally, we will work on strong emotional intentions to infuse your voice with human connection and influence. As previously discussed, your voice is the most effective way to convey emotion. Studies have shown many decisions are based on emotion, even though we may think our rational minds are in charge. Just as great singers can bring an audience to joy or tears at will, you will be able to convince, inspire or educate on a profound level as you decisively choose your intention and result.

Next, we will examine how this amazing instrument works so you can better understand and control your voice.

CHAPTER SEVEN

How Your Voice Works

"There is deep wisdom within our very flesh, if we can only come to our senses and feel it."

– ELIZABETH A. BEHNKE

THE VOCAL TRINITY

The voice is an instrument so complex that we still don't know exactly how everything works. Voice teachers argue about the best ways to breathe or increase range. Voice scientists will debate the acoustic functions of the voice. Even the exact function of all the muscles involved in changing pitch is not completely settled.

But in all this complexity, the voice can be broken down into three main components: Energy, source, and filter. I call this the "vocal trinity." I teach this concept to voice teachers around the world.

Your vocal folds sit at the top of your trachea, housed by the larynx or voice box, and have two main jobs. The first is to help keep food, drink, and other matter, such as saliva, out of your lungs. People often think that if their vocal folds feel dry and scratchy, drinking water will coat and soothe them. However, the water is not supposed to touch your vocal folds; if it does, you immediately start hacking and coughing to get the water out of there - it has gone down the wrong way.

The second job is communication. This is accomplished by the vocal folds coming together and stopping the flow of air from your lungs.

Breathing in and out is mostly silent as the air molecules moving in and out of your lungs are relatively stable in relation to one another. To create sound, we must disturb this relationship and create a miniature weather system.

Weather forcasters talk about high and low pressure zones. These opposing zones create air movement as nature attempts to restore equilibrium (consistent pressure), but nature is not so good at this and over-corrects. These overcorrections give us wind, tornadoes, hurricanes, and sound.

Sound waves are alternating "waves" of high and low pressure. The faster and more extreme the change, the higher and louder the pitch.

To make sound, we need to interrupt the airflow from our lungs and create changes in the air pressure.

So the first part of the vocal trinity is the energy from the lungs. The faster this stream of air, the louder we can get.

But this air is not yet oscillating from low to high pressure. This is the job of the vocal folds. The flow is temporarily blocked when the folds close over this stream of air. (Note: the space between the vocal folds is called the glottis, so this part of the process is glottal closure). As the glottis remains closed, we have rising pressure beneath the vocal folds and dropping pressure above. This starts the weather system. As the folds open and close rapidly (hundreds of times a second), we get rapidly changing pressure. These changes start the air molecules vibrating and banging into their neighboring molecules. This chain of vibrating air travels through your vocal tract (throat and mouth) and past your lips through space to the listener's ears.

The breath is the raw, potential energy, and the folds are the source, the motor which takes the air and turns it into sound.

The final (and most important) part of this process is your vocal tract or filter. Your throat and mouth filter the raw sound waves, enhancing some parts and reducing others. This filtering gives us not only the tone or color of the voice but also vowels and language. It's an essential part of the system.

I will show you how to get these three parts working together to give you efficiency, power, and even beauty. On the flip side, an imbalance in these elements can lead to a poor-sounding voice, fatigue, strain and even damage.

THE BREATH

Breath is the foundation of life, as well as the voice. Developing good breathing habits can also help with mood, energy levels, and overall health.

Our aim is to harness the energy of our breath, managing it as a consistent, steady flow. However, depending on the situation, we may unintentionally underpower our voice with inadequate airflow, or conversely, exert more air than needed.

High-stress situations can throw off our balance of airflow. Stress and anxiety can cause rapid shallow breathing or a holding back of air. Not only do these breathing issues affect the voice, they can also increase the levels of stress and anxiety.

By taking time to work on and connect with your breath, you will be better prepared for a variety of speaking situations, and you might experience additional health benefits as well.

Your breath is powered by, once again, changes in pressure. When you breathe in, your thorax or chest cavity will expand, mainly by the muscles of your ribs lifting them up and out. Your diaphragm will also contract and drop.

The dome-shaped diaphragm muscle lies at the base of your lungs and attaches to them. By contracting and dropping, the diaphragm pulls down on the lungs and expands them. The lungs are also connected to the thorax, and lifting the chest further expands the lungs. This expansion creates a drop in pressure and a vacuum effect pulls air from the outside into the lungs.

The process reverses to exhale. The diaphragm rises and pushes against the bottom of the lungs, and the thorax contracts to further reduce the size of the lungs, pushing out the air within.

This process has a few ways it can go wrong for speakers, especially when we need our voices to carry and fill a room full of listeners.

When we are sleeping or relaxed, there is less movement in the breathing muscles. This passive state is automatic and usually appropriate for our needs (unless we deal with sleep apnea, asthma, etc.).

This passive breathing level is no longer sufficient when speaking in a higher level situation, such as a large meeting or public presentation. The speaker will often start squeezing the vocal folds to get more energy out of a low volume of air. This causes the vocal folds to slam together with excessive force, which can irritate and swell the tissue, leading to vocal fatigue and hoarseness.

Or we might compensate by pulling in too much air; this is not a good solution either. If we overfill the lungs with air, they will rapidly expel the excess when exhaling, much like letting the air out of an overinflated balloon.

This air onslaught can overwhelm the vocal folds, causing them to open too quickly or over-tighten in response, leading to a breathy or an over-tightened, strained voice.

Once you learn to take air in and control its outward flow, you will be able to send the right amount of air to your vocal folds for the current situation. Also, controlled breath can be a powerful asset in controlling nerves in a high-stakes environment.

In my book, *Beginning Singing*, I give breath exercises for singers. These exercises are modified here for speakers. They are simple and efficient. Again, awareness combined with a small amount of application can quickly create positive changes.

EXERCISES

Stand in a tall, "noble" posture.

Keep your chest or thorax feeling open.

As you breathe in, focus on pulling the breath down and around. You will feel your belly drop (down), and the rib cage expand. Don't try and force excess air into your lungs; just take a deep, relaxed breath.

This is your inhalation.

We will next practice a controlled exhale.

Place your hand about two inches below your belly button and give a slight cough. You will feel your lower abdominal muscles "kick out."

Give a few sharp hisses (SSS) and use these muscles to push the air.

Breathe in again, feeling the air drop down to your belly, allowing the ribs to expand again.

Now slowly exhale on a hissing sound (a long, sustained SSS), using the lower abdominal muscles to press out and expel the air.

The chest (or sternum) should remain steady, feeling open in the ribs, even as you breathe out.

This is what singers call "support." The breath supports the voice in a steady stream of controlled air.

Be careful not to over-breathe. The lungs have an amount of elastic recoil, and if you pull in too much air, the lungs will naturally rush it out beyond your control. On the other hand, if you take in a "surprised" breath, it will be plenty. For example, imagine running into an old friend that you haven't seen for a while. The happily surprised breath you naturally take before exclaiming "hello" will be just right.

Singers talk of singing on the inhalation, which of course, is not what they do (unless making an extreme sound known as reverse phonation). Instead, they mean to keep the attitude of breathing in even as the air leaves the lungs, which helps stop the support system from collapsing and the air rushing out too quickly.

I have prepared a video on how to practice breathing in the members' area of this book.

Next, we will look at gaining better control of your vocal folds.

THE VOCAL FOLDS

If we imagine the voice as a combustion engine, your vocal folds are the spark plugs that turn the gas vapor of the breath into energy. Until we engage the folds, we have silent breathing. The action of these two small units of ligament, muscle, and tissue starts the vibration of air. They are quite a remarkable little engine indeed.

The size of vocal folds can greatly differ among individuals, with the level of testosterone exposure often playing a significant role in these variations. This difference in size is a key factor contributing to pitch differences.

Voices that have been influenced by testosterone usually have vocal folds that measure between 17 to 25 millimeters, or about 0.67 to 0.98 inches in length (approximately the diameter of a US nickel to a quarter). This size typically results in a lower pitched voice.

Conversely, voices that have not undergone significant changes from testosterone exposure typically have vocal folds between 12.5 to 17.5 millimeters, or about 0.49 to 0.69 inches in length (roughly the size of a US dime to a nickel). This smaller size usually results in a higher average pitch.

The vocal folds are amazingly small for the amount of range they can produce!

The folds sit at the top of your trachea or windpipe and look like an upside-down V when open, together at the front and apart at the back. This is their position when you breathe.

To make sound, the folds come together at the back and seal over the trachea. Closing the folds during an exhale will interrupt the air flow and cause a change in the air pressure of your vocal tract (throat and mouth). These sudden shifts in pressure start the sound wave. The vocal folds will close, open, and close again hundreds of times a second when making sound.

You can approach a million vocal fold cycles per day if you have a large number of meetings or presentations. So you can imagine what can happen to this delicate tissue if we don't phonate or make sound in a healthy manner.

There is a vast amount of variation that can occur in this sound-making process. The number of times the folds open and close per second will determine the pitch (faster equals higher), but there is another crucial element we want to be aware of.

The energy of the voice (apart from the pitch) is determined by how quickly your folds close and how long they stay closed versus being open. If our folds are opening and closing 200 times per second, there can be a variation in the closed part of the phase versus. the open.

If the folds close briefly and spend most of the phase open, the sound waves will be weak. If they stay closed longer and reduce the open phase, the sound waves will be stronger. Changing the airflow resistance allows you to make the same pitch but with different intensity levels.

We want to balance the amount of air coming to the folds with the amount of vocal fold resistance (staying closed). Not enough resistance, and we are breathy and weak. Too much resistance and we are straining and on our way to vocal fatigue.

We also need the vocal folds to be healthy. Most vocal health protocols focus on keeping the folds flexible, strong, and moist. The outer layer of mucosal tissue is like your inner cheeks. The tissue secretes mucous as a lubricant for the stunningly fast phonation cycles. If this mucous is insufficient or overly thick, we have issues—more on this in the vocal health chapter.

Here are some basic exercises to help your awareness of your vocal folds and to find balanced resistance.

EXERCISES

Start with taking in your supported breath and then making a long, drawn-out sigh. This is insufficient vocal fold closure, with little breath energy being converted into sound.

Now pretend you are lifting some heavy and give a grunt. The result is far too much fold closure and resistance. Speaking this way would tire and even swell the vocal folds from the strain.

Now take in your supported breath and give an enthusiastic "mmmm" like you are eating your absolute favorite food.

This is balanced vocal fold resistance. You will notice you can hold out this "mmmm" for quite a long period of time by sending just enough air to keep this buzzy phonation going. This balance is how singers can hold notes for what seems like an impossible amount of time.

Alternate between practicing the breath on a hiss and then on the hum. Watch the hum does not get breathy or squeezed sounding.

It may take a bit of practice to find the balance of airflow vs. resistance, but it will soon be second nature.

RESONANCE

Vocal resonance is the magic of the voice, where the sound waves are reinforced, filtered, and turned into power, tone color, and even language.

Imagine clapping your hands in a closet full of clothes versus a giant cathedral—the same pair of clapping hands but a very different sonic result. The cathedral enhances the initial "clap" in a more dynamic way by reflecting the sound waves. Resonance is a similar reflection or echo in your vocal tract.

Resonance provides the building of power for your voice. It is how opera singers can be heard over a large orchestra without the help of a microphone. The resonance potential within your vocal tract can turn your voice from a cheap radio to an audiophile stereo system.

The secret is how you shape your vocal tract. Think of a pipe organ. You can look at the pipes and know which ones are for the low notes and which are for the higher pitches. Low notes resonate better in a larger space, and high frequencies need smaller spaces.

Your vocal tract is capable of containing many different pipes at the same time due to its complexity and flexibility. It's the difference between the organ playing a single low or high note or a chord consisting of a series of pitches simultaneously.

If your voice is thin, over-bright, dull, and lacking vibrancy, this is like the organ playing a single note. We want a lush chord of low and high notes. Low and high notes at the same time? Isn't the voice only capable of one pitch at a time?

Well, yes and no. Although we can only speak or sing on one pitch at a time, these pitches or vocal sounds have a full spectrum of sounds (or potential sounds) within them. Almost all sounds are complex, containing many individual pitches or partials. These partials give instruments not only pitch but also color. The complexity of these micro-pitches makes a trumpet sound different from a trombone. They are also a big part of why you sound like you and no one else.

The sound waves from the vocal folds are a kaleidoscope of these micro-pitches, full of lower and higher frequencies. If left as is, we would not have understandable language or pitch; it would be "pink noise," somewhat like the sound of waves on the beach.

Your vocal tract filters and aligns all these partials of the sound waves into a more ordered and musical sound. It can also change the color and tone of your voice. This filtering is known as "resonance."

The interaction of sound waves in your vocal tract is so remarkable that voice researchers are not yet settled on exactly how this happens.

I will take you through a short series of exercises to first increase your awareness of resonance and then start controlling it to dial in your best vocal sound.

Come back to these exercises often, as resonance is arguably the most crucial part of your voice.

EXERCISES

Just as we did with the previous vocal fold exercises, make a robust "mmmm" like you are eating your favorite food.

Now hold out the NG sound of "suNG." You will notice your tongue is up against your soft palate. Make this area the focus of your attention. As you hold the NG sound, feel the vibrations in your soft palate.

Hold the NG again and slide up and down on the pitch like a slow siren.

What changes with the vibration sensation as the pitch changes? You will likely feel the vibration sensation lift into your head slightly as if the sound is starting to go behind your eyes.

This change in sensation is what singers refer to as head voice. The feeling of lifting vibrations is the body experiencing and absorbing part of these faster vibrating sound waves. Yes, the body absorbs much of the sound we make, in fact, MOST of the sound, but not to worry, there is still plenty of energy left to go out to our listener's ears.

Stay with the NG and glide up again. This time, when you reach a higher pitch, drop your tongue and exclaim AH!. The sensation should be bright and buzzy.

Stay on this note and exclaim HOHO, HAHA, and then HEHE.

The energy of the voice should feel lifted and vital. Let the breath drive the sound rather than your vocal folds.

I've prepared a video that takes you through this sequence in the members' area of the book (compellingspeakerbook.com).

YOUR BEST VOICE

When you get the three elements of the voice working together (your breath, vocal folds, and resonance), you will have an instrument (yes, instrument) of beauty and power.

Your breath will supply a steady flow of air to your vocal folds. The folds will close over and turn this flow of air into acoustic energy. Your vocal tract will filter and enhance this energy into wonderfully complex and rich sound waves that will carry and fill the space in which you are speaking.

As you gain awareness and facility with your voice, it will be more flexible and varied, able to adapt to the situation. Your voice can carry a presentation with vibrancy and confidence and become warm and nurturing when helping a colleague or employee.

Now that we are developing a great sounding instrument, let's make some music with it!

CHAPTER EIGHT

Your Musical Voice

"Music is the shorthand of emotion."
– LEO TOLSTOY

W hat came first, singing or speech? It's a proverbial chicken vs. egg debate. It appears they developed in tandem with each other, which I believe is important to keep in mind. Some anthropologists and evolutionary biologists have hypothesized that a form of "musical protolanguage" might have been the first form of human communication before the development of fully articulated speech. This hypothesis, known as the "musilanguage" model, proposes that early human communication was a mixture of melodic intonation and rhythmically produced sounds that communicated emotions more than concepts. Over time, this musilanguage would have gradually evolved into more complex forms of both music and speech.

One of my missions is to connect people to their singing past, something we have lost in more recent modern societies.

In the late 19th and early 20th centuries, the piano was a staple in middle-class homes, especially in the US and Europe. Gathering around and making music was the entertainment of the day, and singing was a large part of it.

The rise of the radio and phonograph changed this dynamic. Music went from an active to a passive event, and we could now have world-class professional singers reproduced in our homes on demand.

People started to believe singing is for professionals. "I can't sing" or "I have a terrible voice" became a common excuse. An unfortunate side effect was that musicality began to fade from our speaking voices.

Singing and speech are a rich part of our evolutionary history, and music is a primal communicator of emotion. When you bring melody and music to your voice, the brain can't help but light up in recognition and engagement.

I'm not looking to turn you into a singer, but I want to show you how to access the same devices great singers use to captivate and even emotionally manipulate their audiences. Experienced performers know what reactions a song will elicit. They know which notes and words will grab the audience, and they have ways to maximize the impact. Singers know how to get specific emotional reactions from the listener, a form of pleasant manipulation.

I will give you musical devices to help you become a vocal performer who knows how and when to hit the "money notes" with your audience.

HOW SINGERS HOLD AN AUDIENCE

The singer before me was experiencing a host of vocal issues. It was our first lesson together and I was going through the process of analyzing and assessing the voice to discover the root causes of the issues and how I could best help.

Her voice was raspy from overuse and fatigue and the voice was cracking as she tried to sing higher notes. A lot of work to be done indeed.

She had a high-profile performance coming up that would be attended by a number of music industry types, and she was understandably nervous. I asked her to sing the song she would be performing.

Suddenly, the issues fell into the background and I was transported by her musicality and artistry. She would vary her tone and intensity as she came to the different sections of the song. When words and melody were repeated, she employed new variations of rhythm and phrasing to make everything sound brand new. It was a masterclass in musicianship.

Yes, her voice still had problems, but her ability to incorporate musical devices along with emotional honesty had me nearly in tears by the end of the song.

It was a reminder that it's not only the sound of the voice, but how musical you are that counts.

These same powerful elements are available to you.

Popular music contains a lot of repetition; that's part of its appeal. By having repeated verses and choruses, the song is catchy and memorable. The secret is introducing new elements within the repetition to hold the listener's interest.

A song containing too much new information can sound confusing (or some may joke, like jazz). However, if the music is too predictable (think "Three Blind Mice"), then it sounds rote and boring with little reason to continue listening.

In speech, too much variation is undesirable as it can make us sound unhinged, but rote speech that falls into predictable patterns can be excruciating to sit through.

Great songwriting and production consistently add new elements as a song progresses. Some are obvious, such as a large choir coming in on the last chorus, but many changes are incredibly subtle, a shaker now adding to the rhythm or a second layer of guitar.

Singers will do the same: big changes such as long sustains, but also small shifts that grab and hold your interest.

These shifts can include playing with the tempo, speeding up, or slowing down a line—changes in tone from brighter to darker, or placing accents and stresses in new places.

By not delivering on every expectation, the singer creates small surprises that reawaken interest.

The number of variations a singer may employ is vast and varied, but there are key elements most singers use. I will show you the most effective ones here.

There is an ongoing debate on the effect of digital media on the average attention span, with many believing it has gotten shorter. By discovering and implementing these musical devices, you stand a great chance of reaching your listener.

A musical voice is a more compelling voice.

OPTIMAL SPEAKING PITCH

One lesson I would like you to take away from reading this book is finding your OSP. Discovering where your voice works best can help with tone, fatigue, power, and overall health.

As previously discussed, many of us mistake a rich authoritative voice with speaking at a lower pitch.

As we will see, the depth and richness of your voice will come from developing your full spectrum of resonance. Pitch and resonance are different, although they are often perceptually conflated. I have a video demonstrating the difference in the member's area.

While speaking at too high of a pitch is an obvious issue, it is somewhat rare. First, an overly high pitch is instantly noticeable, and the speaker will likely take steps on their own to correct it. However, if this is an issue for you, the following exercises will also work for you.

The more common issue is speaking too low. While some of us have a naturally lower voice, most are likely under where the voice should naturally be.

When we center our voice on a range that is too low, we lose energy, making the vocal folds work too hard. The extra effort can lead to fatigue and swelling, lowering the pitch even more.

I have helped speakers quickly eliminate vocal fatigue with these simple exercises.

I received a call to travel to a hotel room where a famous sports announcer was staying. He was in town for a game and was experiencing extreme fatigue with his voice. When I arrived, the scene was slightly chaotic with assistants handing him notes as he was reviewing video of the teams who would be playing that day.

I only had a brief period of time to work with him, so I focused on his speaking pitch, which had dropped below his optimal level, causing his voice to work too hard.

Within minutes he rediscovered where his voice should be. I gave him exercises to keep his voice healthy and how to vocalize through a straw (more on that later). As I left, he was raving to his assistant how much better his voice felt. Speaking at your optimal pitch can solve a host of issues.

Finding your OSP is relatively easy; the work comes in creating awareness and habit.

When I first started teaching voice full-time, I was not paying attention to the pitch of my voice. Voice lessons can be pretty intense for the teacher, with demonstrating, correcting, and explaining adding up to a fair amount of voice use.

I was getting to the end of my teaching days vocally exhausted, which surprised me because I was an experienced singer who could do gigs and shows without issues. My voice felt fine when singing, but I could feel the fatigue creeping in when I would talk.

In my search for a solution, I came across the concept of OSP in an older book called *Change Your Voice, Change Your Life* by Dr. Morton Cooper. I realized that I was speaking relatively low in my voice, causing fatigue. I did a few simple exercises to recalibrate my voice and then made it my mission to create a new vocal habit.

Each time my phone would ring (yes, this was back when we would answer our phones), I would reset my pitch and vocal energy before answering. Likewise, I would conduct a silent mental reboot before engaging in face-to-face conversations.

I quickly developed a new speaking habit and would end my teaching days with my voice still feeling great.

On extended teaching days, or when I was physically fatigued, it became necessary to pay extra attention to my voice to prevent it from dropping in pitch. With this approach, I managed to maintain my vocal quality even on the most demanding days.

Each singer has an area of the voice where it works best. Singers will often change the key of a song (move the whole song higher or lower) to sit in the right spot of the voice. This is also where the concept of voice classification comes in (i.e., tenor vs. a baritone). A tenor's vocal "sweet spot" will sit higher than a baritone's.

Finding your OSP is like finding the right song key or voice classification. Don't get stuck wondering if you are a soprano or an alto; allow sensation and sound quality to guide you.

Here are the steps to finding your OSP. I have also prepared a step-by-step video for you in the members' area.

EXERCISES

Say "mmm hmmm" like you enthusiastically agree with something.

You should hear the pitch rise at the end of this.

Now hold the higher pitch for a few seconds. It should feel buzzy, vibrating your nose and the front of your mouth.

Move this pitch up and down slightly to find the maximum spot of vibration and resonance.

Start a hum on this pitch and then move into an emotionally positive phrase, such as "Yes, that's right!" or "Absolutely!"

The pitch of these phrases should be your OSP area. It may take a bit of getting used to as it is likely higher than where you usually speak. Finally, your OSP is not rigid; it is more like a home base for your voice. We certainly don't want to limit our speaking to just one or even just a few pitches. We want to use our OSP as the center of a wider array of pitches. This spectrum of notes is known as vocal range.

RANGE

A singer's range is their lowest usable low note to their highest. I say usable because our range can change from morning to evening as the vocal folds change. Usable range is where the voice is consistent and reliable rather than the extremes.

While speakers do not want or need to access all the notes a singer employs, we want to increase our available range. By working on range, you will keep the ligaments and muscles of the voice agile and strong and the tissues of the folds healthy.

Like the rest of the body, the voice will become progressively weak and stiff as we age. A loss of range is one of the more noticeable effects (along with a change in average speaking pitch). By working on and employing more range in the voice, you can help slow the aging process and keep a youthful sparkle in the voice.

A flexible, accessible range will allow melody in the voice. Melody can have a significant effect on the listener.

It's believed that varying pitches can activate different regions of the brain associated with auditory processing and emotional interpretation. The science suggests that a speaker using a wide range of pitches could stimulate a broader network of regions in a listener's brain than a monotonous speaker, potentially leading to more engagement and deeper processing of the spoken content.

In other words, sing a song people will want to listen to.

Here are a few exercises to help you develop and access more range in your voice.

EXERCISES:

Make a joyful whooping sound, "woo-hoo!"

Do this again and allow the OO sounds to float into your upper range. The higher notes can be tricky initially, as the voice muscles may want to over-engage and tighten up. Let the "woo-hoo" be light, like a hooty-sounding falsetto.

Now say a firm AH at the lower part of your range.

Next, glide from the low AH up to a high OO.

Repeat this a few times to access the full extent of your vocal range.

Daily exercises can help grow your available range and make your voice more flexible.

TONE

Tone refers to the color, timbre, the very sound of your voice. Tone is tied to and controlled by resonance, which is controlled by the shaping of your vocal tract.

The other essential element of great tone is the creation of the sound wave itself. Again, the sound wave impulse results from the vocal folds interrupting airflow from the lungs. This interruption creates imbalances in air pressure, and this causes the air molecules in your vocal tract to begin vibrating. However, not all vibrations are the same.

If we don't get a balanced level of vocal fold resistance to the airflow, we can end up with weak, breathy sound waves or pressed, overly harsh sound waves.

No amount of shaping from the vocal tract will overcome a poorly produced sound wave. We want to ensure our folds and air give us the best raw materials possible.

Be sure to go back and review the exercises in the Vocal Folds chapter.

I also encourage you to go back occasionally and reconnect with the sensations of resonance. You will have access to the full range of expressive sounds by controlling your air, vocal fold, and resonance.

Vocal tone is a near-infinite kaleidoscope of colors. While we practice eliminating breathiness or harsher tones, this does not mean you should never use them. They are part of the emotional landscape of the voice, reflecting emotions such as compassion or anger. But we want to make sure these extremes are not our default.

Between the extremes of the voice is a wide variety of sounds. You do not need to use most of them in an average conversation. But, as the stage you are on gets larger or the stakes increase, these elements can be powerful.

Play is essential to learning to be more musical with your voice. While you have used different colors and tones in your speech, it has likely not been in your conscious awareness. You have probably not played with your voice since childhood.

Let's explore the various colors your voice can make.

EXERCISES:

Place your fingers on your larynx (or voice box). The larynx is felt as the bump in the front middle of your neck that goes up and down when you swallow. The protrusion is also commonly known as the Adam's apple.

Take fast, shallow breaths, like a dog panting, and feel where your larynx is. Now take a deep, relaxed breath. Did the position change? You likely felt the larynx higher on the shallow breaths and lower on the deeper ones.

Return to the shallow, high larynx position and say, "Nice to meet you!" You will notice a thin, bright sound due to the shape of the vocal tract. The raising of the larynx has shortened the distance from your vocal folds to your lips, changing the timbre or tone of your voice by emphasizing the higher frequencies of the sound wave.

Now go to the deep relaxed breaths position, feel the larynx drop, and say the same phrase. Don't try and change the pitch at your vocal folds, only your larynx. The sound will be deeper and richer because of the longer vocal tract.

Changing the length of the vocal tract is often used by cartoon voice actors. SpongeBob and Patrick (two favorites of mine) are examples of high and low larynx positions.

The next two levers we can play with for tone are the lips.

Say "Nice to meet you" in your current "normal" voice. Now round your lips in an OO shape and say the phrase while keeping the lips rounded. This shape creates a darker tone but is less dull than a low larynx.

Now widen your lips into a broad smile and repeat the phrase. It will now be brighter but in a different way from the high larynx.

Play with mixing and matching your larynx and lips combinations. Read a sentence on this page and alternate the words between bright and dark colors. Now reread the sentence and drop the exaggerations but keep a sense of changing color in your speech. As you play with this, going from exaggerations to a heightened tonal sense of "regular" speaking, you will find new colors coming into your voice.

DYNAMICS

Dynamics refer to musical changes in amplitude or volume and are a powerful way to create variety in your voice. You can use dynamics to build to an important point or drop into a quiet tone to pull and focus the listener's attention.

Contrasts are crucial to holding attention. Listen to a great vocal performance; you will hear varying vocal intensity and dynamics, building and pulling back, layering and heightening emotion and musical phrases.

Dynamics have direct emotional effect. We have a natural flow in the dynamics of most heightened communication. Speaking without dynamic contrasts can sound rote and dry.

By utilizing dynamics, you can create suspense or anticipation in your talk. A rise in volume alerts the listener that we are building to something; pulling back can drop the tension and create a sense of ease.

Dynamics can convey emotions effectively. Soft speech can express sadness, introspection, or calmness, while a louder voice can bring excitement, anger, or urgency. This emotional engagement can make you more relatable and impactful.

ACCENTS

While dynamics usually refer to longer sections of music, we can also quickly change volume and place stresses on certain words.

These stresses are dynamic changes that make words pop for emphasis. These stresses or accents ("accent" in music means a note louder than the neighboring notes, not to be confused with a speaking accent) are also important for communication and intention.

For example, say the following sentence out loud, but each time, emphasize a different word:

HE never said she stole my money.

He NEVER said she stole my money.

He never SAID she stole my money.

He never said SHE stole my money.

He never said she STOLE my money.

He never said she stole MY money.

He never said she stole my MONEY.

The sentence can have seven different meanings and inferences simply by changing the stressed word.

Accents also give your speech rhythm and propulsion, which is essential to music.

Try clapping your hands with a steady beat (like the ticking of a stopwatch). Not a very interesting sound.

Now begin emphasizing some claps over others, making them a little louder. You will notice it starts to sound more rhythmic and musical. These accents are incredibly effective in making what you have to say more interesting.

Rap artists are masters of using accents to create incredibly complex rhythms and musical propulsion.

I suggest playing with these accents using text or points from a recent meeting or talk. Infuse your words with rap-styled rhythms and accents. Then move into natural speech but keep a sense of these rhythms and accents.

You will start to find your own unique flow and propulsions, which will allow you to create more interest when speaking.

TEMPO

While rhythm is the subdivision and propulsion of speech, tempo is the overall pace. Why are sad songs generally slow and happy party songs uptempo? Because much of music is connected to the human voice and the spoken word. We naturally speak slower when sad and faster when happy or excited.

By varying the tempo of your voice, you control the emotional flow as well. While most modern popular music has the same tempo from beginning to end, classical composers understood the range and depth of emotion they could elicit from varying tempos.

You can create your own symphony with varying movements and emotions by utilizing tempo changes, along with rhythmic accents and dynamics.

It is natural to speak faster when getting to an exciting point or to slow down in more mundane moments during a presentation, but these are not hard rules. You have the freedom to play with tempo. Consider introducing a sense of suspense by deliberately slowing down during intense segments or breathe new life into the less dynamic sections by picking up the pace. In essence, the tempo of your speech is an element you can change to enrich the impact of your communication.

Tempo is one of your most powerful speaking tools, and it is where I see a significant number of speaking mistakes.

If we are nervous about giving a presentation, we will tend to talk faster. This non-stop rush of words can be hard to follow and unnerving for the listener. After a few rushed talks, we tell ourselves to slow down. The result is a slow, ponderous slog that is difficult for the listener.

What you want is a controlled variation in tempo. If I give a talk and notice the audience's attention slipping, I know to create variations as a pattern interrupt. I will change my tempo of speech instantly. This shift is often enough to reengage attention. Add in dynamics, rhythm, and tone, and you have an unending number of vocal combinations to hold interest.

EXERCISES:

Remember the rules of a great song--the combination of the familiar and the unfamiliar. If we overdo these elements, we can sound distracted or unhinged.

Take a piece of text and play with varying tempos.

Once again, this is a time to have fun and be silly.

Alternately speed up and slow down, exaggerate this at first and then become more subtle.

Pay attention to how it affects the energy of the text.

Now try this on a talk or meeting point. Play with the tempo and notice the changes.

The key to this exercise is awareness and listening.

Ultimately, we don't want to overdo tempo. It is a device to be used carefully, but creating a heightened sense of tempo and its effect is often enough to break us out of static, rote habits of speaking at one rate of speed.

In the next chapter we will combine all our musical elements together and SING!

CHAPTER NINE

Finding Your Inner Music

"Music is the divine way to tell beautiful,
poetic things to the heart."

– PABLO CASALS

N ow it's time to play, have a little fun. You might find these exercises a bit intimidating, especially if it's been a while since you permitted yourself to sing, to enjoy the vibrations of your voice. Singing is our birthright and a means of communication that dates back to our first utterances, both as infants and the ancient beginnings of the human race.

It is rare to meet someone who doesn't harbor a secret desire to be able to sing. I believe this desire is born within us as social beings. We all know the beauty of emotions music brings us, and we naturally want to connect with others in this way.

As discussed previously, pianos and singing were once the centerpiece of household entertainment, until the radio and phonograph turned music into a passive event to be done by professionals.

Great athletes like Tiger Woods did not stop people from enjoying golf; he brought more people to the game. However, singing feels very personal, and there is unnecessary embarrassment or even shame if we don't sing at the level of a skilled professional.

I want to change this attitude for you. If you wish to be a great communicator, reconnect with the music inside you.

I ask my clients to play a game I call "the world's worst musical." This is an exercise in being wholly free and silly.

Find an area where you feel safe, where others cannot hear you. Take a section of a talk or points of an upcoming meeting and sing what you will say. And I mean, sing the words as silly as you like!

Don't feel the need to sound good; that will likely bring self-judgment and intimidation. Allow yourself to sound "bad."

Try singing the words with different approaches. Make the song a fast up-tempo high-energy number, then try a mellow ballad. Do corny, over-the-top musical theater, anything that makes you stretch and play with your voice.

Then, move from singing to speaking and then back to singing again. Do this in one constant motion. As you move to "speaking," I want you to keep an attitude of singing throughout. Find the music in your speaking voice.

Move back and forth in this way until you can feel the music pulsing in your speech.

The next element will unite your musical devices in a natural and impactful flow. We will learn the power of emotional intentions.

CHAPTER TEN

Emotional Intentions

"Feelings or emotions are the universal language and are to be honored. They are the authentic expression of who you are at your deepest place."
– JUDITH WRIGHT

We've all heard singers with excellent technique--beautiful tone, soaring high notes--but who, in the end, leave us emotionally cold.

It all sounds great, but something is missing. They don't create that vital connection to our human core.

Then there are singers without perfect voices, yet we feel the passion and truth pulsating in their voices.

I tell my singing clients that technique is merely a tool rather than the highest level of singing.

We want solid vocal techniques to keep our voices healthy, vibrant, and being heard, but we still need to SAY something; we need to use the voice at its highest level. And that level is emotional connection and communication.

By drawing from the world of acting, we can discover techniques that assist us in establishing these crucial connections.

To create emotional authenticity, actors will use what are referred to as objectives and intentions.

Every time we speak to someone, we want something. These wants can be macro or micro.

If your ultimate goal is to sell something to a client, that is your objective, your macro "want."

In trying to achieve this larger objective, you will employ intentions. Intentions are acting verbs, breaking down what you want in each moment, and intentions will often change throughout the flow of conversation or a presentation, even though the ultimate objective remains the same.

You might start the conversation with a small joke or observation. Your intention in doing this is "to amuse." You may ask about their family. Your intention in doing so might be "to connect."

As your meeting moves along, you will ask about the issues they face that your product or service can solve (to inquire). You then talk about your solution (to instruct) and how it can make this client's life easier (to inspire).

We use intentions constantly, though we are not usually aware of them. However, intentions are incredibly powerful and can be used to ignite your voice with passion and authority.

When giving a public talk, intentions can help focus and create an emotional flow. A mistake speakers often make is to force an emotion on the situation (I'm going to be excited"). These forced emotions rarely work as they often come off as inauthentic.

In a scene where a character receives terrible news, the actor will not choose to be "sad" or "angry." Instead, they will make strong intentional choices such as "to rebuke," "to deny," "to plead." These intentions, what this character WANTS in this moment, will create and drive natural emotion.

Instead of forcing an emotion, create a flow of intentions for your talk.

When walking out and greeting the audience, a chance for connection is often lost. The speaker will treat the "hello" as a formality with their thoughts on what they will say (or worse, turning inward with self-doubt and anxiety).

What if your intention was TO EMBRACE? Don't worry about what they think about you or if you are projecting the right energy; take a beat and fully embrace the room. How would that change the opening of your talk?

Would your body language be more open? Would you make engaging eye contact? Would you stop a beat and smile? And would this deep intention of embracing this room be reflected in the very vibrations of your voice?

What would the audience's experience be like? We've all felt the energy when a charismatic person walks on stage. But what is genuine charisma? Is it a forced smile and energy? No, we naturally recoil from fake emotions.

True charisma is someone who walks out and fills the room with honest and true emotional energy, not something manufactured.

If your one intention in the moment is to embrace truly, then the audience will sense and feel it. As you talk, your voice will impart this honest emotional intention, resulting in "charisma."

As your talk flows, you can have a number of intentions. As you hint at a payoff reveal, you want "to tease" or "entice."

You list essential points; your intention is "to educate" or "inform."

You give optimistic sales projections; your intention is "to inspire" or "celebrate."

The stronger and more concrete your intention is within you, the more it will reverberate and fill the room. The universe is vibration; your voice is vibration, and emotional energy is vibration.

The brain of the listener also vibrates. The frequencies of your wonderfully produced musical voice brimming with emotional information create vibration in the neurons. You will literally "vibe" with your listeners.

And as you reveal your true emotional self, you will feel the vibration of the audience coming back towards you, and you will experience true confidence.

It's a beautiful circle of energy exchange, and emotional intentions are key to this connection.

CHOOSING INTENTIONS

The wonderful thing about intentions is how varied you can be with them. The crucial point is that they are actionable and connect to your goal at that moment.

You can incorporate multiple intentions into your presentation or choose to focus on just a few. I recommend starting with a simple approach to get a feel for this technique and then gradually exploring more variations.

Let's start with a few sentences or a paragraph of a talk or meeting you have led. As you look over these words, ask yourself, "What do I want in this moment? What is my goal in saying these words?"

For instance, if you are leading a sales meeting to introduce a new package offering, your larger goal is likely to increase sales, but that is not why you have called a meeting; otherwise, you could simply say, "Sell more of these."

You will have a more specific, immediate goal in this moment and every subsequent moment. The goals will give you intentions.

These intentions can be simple and direct or more abstract and emotional. It's all about your goal.

Take your goal and put it in an actable sentence. I want to (PLACE GOAL HERE). The "I want to" is essential. It drives the action, which causes the natural emotional responses within us.

For instance, when introducing the new sales package, I don't want to start talking without a goal, or my voice can be flat without emotional energy. I also don't want to pick an emotion, like "excitement," because that's a passive word with nothing to drive me to that result.

Instead of thinking "excitement," I choose this as my goal: I want TO EXCITE! The word "to" starts the engine and drives the energy. It gives us an actionable goal.

Let's take this hypothetical opening to a sales meeting:

> I'm excited to be here with you today to share some news that is a game-changer for our business. We've developed a new package of services, designed with our customers' diverse needs in mind. This is the result of our ongoing efforts to stay tuned in to what our customers require, and to innovate our services accordingly.
>
> Over the next three weeks, we have a task ahead of us. We need to communicate the merits of this new package effectively to our customers. This isn't just another product to sell, it's a thoughtfully designed package that can significantly enhance our customers' experience with us.

Now let's choose some possible intentions. Remember, there is no correct answer, and you can change your intentions at any time.

Reread the first paragraph and answer, "What is my goal here? What do I want to achieve?"

> *I'm excited to be here with you today to share some news that is a game-changer for our business. We've developed a new package of services, designed with our customers' diverse needs in mind. This is the result of our ongoing efforts to stay tuned in to what our customers require, and to innovate our services accordingly.*

Some intentions I come up with are: to reveal, inspire, excite, motivate, explain.

Now some of these goals are very close to each other, at least at first glance. The difference between inspire and motivate appears small; the words are nearly interchangeable. That is until you use them as intentions.

Each intention will manifest differently from person to person and even sentence to sentence.

Say this next paragraph out loud while thinking: "I want to motivate." Picture this imaginary sales team becoming inspired into action by your words. Feel your desire for this result as you speak the words aloud.

> *Over the next three weeks, we have a task ahead of us. We need to communicate the merits of this new package effectively to our customers. This isn't just another product to sell, it's a thoughtfully designed package that can significantly enhance our customers' experience with us.*

Note how that felt.

Now choose to inspire. How does someone who is inspired look and feel different from motivated? Is there a different energy?

Visualize this group full of inspiration. Feel how much you want them to be inspired.

Now reread the words. Let your voice feel and express this desire within you.

Was there a different feel and energy? Was the music of your voice different?

Intentions do not need to be as emotionally charged as these examples. You could also choose something more low-key, such as "to explain."

While explaining is not as charged a goal as inspiring, it is still a goal and should receive the same focus. Make the intention "to explain" and visualize your words being heard and understood.

Speak the same words with explaining as your focused goal.

How was that different? What's different about your energy and voice?

While the energy may have changed and perhaps downshifted, it did not go away. It likely became more subtle but still effective.

Intentions can become more natural and second nature with practice.

CREATE YOUR SONG

Emotional intentions serve as the glue that binds the musical elements we've learned. While we'll work on these components individually, the ultimate goal is to ensure our speech doesn't come across as contrived outside the practice room.

When in performance mode, a singer does not focus on the many different parts of being musical; instead, they allow emotion (and the music) to guide their choices, creating a performance that feels honest and spontaneous.

Broadway performers have to do eight shows a week, and yes, it's as difficult and demanding as it sounds. The process of mounting a show involves numerous technical choices and requirements, but once they are in performance, the emotion keeps everything fresh and vital.

We want to infuse our musical voice with our emotional intentions to bring everything we have been working on to life.

Let's revisit the "world's worst musical" exercise in a new way. Take a portion of your talk with your predetermined intention, but now express it in song. Create a "song" that reflects your intention.

Let the intention drive the tempo, the melody, the rhythms, the tone; everything born from what you feel inside, stemming from your very clear goal.

Repeat this a few times and drop all judgment. Experience what it is like to allow emotion and melody to come together. This is the true music of the voice.

If you let go of self-consciousness and allow yourself to feel the music, your emotional intentions should become brighter and intensified.

Now move back and forth from singing to talking, allowing the music to lift and flow through your speech.

Take your time with this, as this synthesis of music, emotion, and communication is the magic. The ability to conjure this level of communication at will is an advantage in persuasion and connection very few of your competitors will have even considered.

You'll learn how to boost connectivity instantly, in a way that feels genuine because it will always stem from honesty. Keep in mind, it's our voice that truly expresses our emotions - it's the primary means by which we grasp each other's feelings.

As you become more comfortable with accessing this higher level of communication, I suggest you employ it throughout your day. When the situation arises where you need to be heard, allow an intention to come to the fore and gently infuse your voice. Open your awareness and energy to encompass your conversation partners and form a genuine connection.

By doing this, you're reaching back to timeless, deeply-rooted communication techniques that will resonate with your listener in unique and unexpected ways.

In the next chapter, we'll explore how to maintain your voice's health, ensuring your communication skills don't just resonate, but also endure.

CHAPTER ELEVEN

Vocal Health

"It is health that is the real wealth and not pieces of gold and silver."

– MAHATMA GANDHI

Just like your body, your voice is built to stand the test of time. Yet, it's often easier to recognize when we've neglected our physical health--the evidence is visible and tangible.

The voice does not give off the same alarm bells. We may not notice our pitch has dropped slightly or our tone is less focused and crisp. The constant clearing of the throat might be more noticeable to others than ourselves.

The vocal folds are selective in the sensory feedback they give us--we certainly don't want to be distracted by the sensations of the folds opening and closing hundreds of times per second. This lack of sensation often means we don't feel the damage we may be doing until it's too late.

What can we do to keep our voice healthy and strong?

Besides good vocal technique, the voice thrives on sleep. Sleep is when the body repairs tissue and engages in cellular regeneration. Sleep also has anti-inflammatory benefits, which is essential for a healthy voice.

Speaking on inflamed vocal folds is like trying to play the trumpet with swollen lips; it doesn't work so well. When your folds swell from overuse and fatigue, you cannot get efficient fold closure to create the sound wave. Your resulting voice will be weaker and less pleasant to listen to.

Another essential element is hydration. Your voice is like an engine, and it needs lubrication. Opening and closing dry vocal folds hundreds of times a second can create irritation.

Hydration will also help eliminate thick mucus on the folds. This mucus can interfere with your voice and usually leads to harsh throat clearing (more on that in a bit).

When the voice is not properly hydrated, we encounter another issue--phonation threshold pressure or PTP. PTP refers to the amount of pressure needed to start the vocal folds phonating or making sound. We want this PTP value to be as low as possible for the chosen vocal intensity.

Drier folds have a higher PTP.

Try this: get your lips moist and buzz them like you are playing the trumpet. Make a mental note of how much air you need to push to get the lips buzzing.

Now wipe your lips dry and try again. You will notice it takes more effort to get the lips buzzing, and it is also a bit more difficult to control.

The same thing happens with your voice. A dry voice takes more muscle and pressure to create sound, which leads to quicker vocal fatigue.

While there is no agreement on how much water you should drink, a common guideline is to aim for an average daily intake of about 8 cups or 2 liters of water for adults. This is often referred to as the "8x8 rule" (eight 8-ounce glasses of water).

However, this is a general recommendation, and individual needs may differ. Listening to your body's thirst signals and ensuring that your urine is pale yellow or clear are good indicators of adequate hydration.

Water intake can also come from other sources such as fruits, vegetables, and other beverages. These contribute to overall hydration levels.

You also want to be careful about eating too close to your bedtime, especially if you have an important vocal day coming up. Going to bed with a full stomach can increase the likelihood of acid reflux (also known as GERD). This can be made even worse by consuming alcohol as it will help relax the lower esophageal sphincter, a muscular ring that normally prevents stomach contents from flowing backward.

Stomach acid coming up the esophagus can burn and irritate the vocal folds. A few drops are enough to take you out of your best voice.

Thick mucus can happen because of hydration issues, but also age. One of the reasons for this thickening is the decrease in moisture content. Aging can reduce the production of natural lubrication in the respiratory tract, including the vocal folds,resulting in thicker mucus that may feel more sticky or difficult to clear.

Additionally, lifestyle factors such as smoking, exposure to dry or polluted environments, and certain medical conditions can further contribute to the thickening of mucus.

Humidifying the air in your environment, especially in dry climates or during winter months, can also help add moisture to the respiratory system.

You can also talk to your doctor about using over-the-counter medications such as guaifenesin to help with mucus issues.

Speaking of doctors, a good ear, nose, and throat doctor is indispensable for professional voice users (and if your income depends on your voice, you are a professional voice user). Even better is a laryngologist, an ENT with a further specialty in the voice.

These voice specialists can diagnose and help treat persistent issues. If you have a voice problem that lingers beyond a cold or flu or a hoarse tired voice that doesn't clear up after a week, seek a voice specialist.

I finally want to talk about a big no-no in the voice, but one you likely do--throat clearing. Throat clearing is a natural reflex to the accumulation of mucus on the folds but doing it harshly or excessively can further irritate the voice and cause more phlegm.

While excessive throat clearing can be a sign of underlying voice issues, for which you should seek medical advice, I want to show you how to clear your throat without causing further irritation.

Instead of slamming the vocal folds together and forcing air through, say a long "who" in a loud whisper (holding out the OO). Then tuck your chin and swallow. This should help get the phlegm off the folds without irritation. I have provided a video example in the members' area for this book.

Many vocal issues are caused by this excessive pressing on the folds, particularly swelling and fatigue. Unchecked, this abuse of the folds can cause them to thicken, much like a callus on the hands. These are known as vocal nodules and these thickened areas can stop the vocal folds from vibrating properly. It can also cause polyps, which are fluid-filled growths on the folds. While nodules can be treated with vocal rest and therapy, polyps usually require surgery.

Nodules and polyps will often show up in the voice as a hoarseness or raspiness that doesn't go away. If you have issues lasting more than two weeks, please seek out a qualified ENT.

A combination of healthy speaking techniques, hydration, diet, and a healthy lifestyle will keep your voice going for a lifetime.

WARMING UP

Warming up the voice before extensive use is like warming up the body before exercise. It helps prepare the vocal folds and other components of the voice for the demands that will be placed on them.

Warm-ups need not take long; a few minutes is usually sufficient. However, if the voice is tired or feeling swollen or hoarse, extra time may be needed.

Remember that your vocal folds will be opening and closing hundreds of times each second. The folds should be properly hydrated and well-rested with a good night's sleep.

As we begin to warm up the voice, we will increase blood flow to the folds. This will get them better prepared for the physical task ahead.

The warm-up routine will also help reduce vocal fold swelling and stiffness in the muscles and ligaments. Remember, your folds are ligament, muscle, and tissue. The ligaments and muscles need flexibility to access the full range and expressiveness of your voice while the tissue needs to be pliable and responsive to create the sound waves.

Your breathing system and support also require engagement at a heightened level. Warm-up exercises get the whole body relaxed and primed for efficient work.

We are also working on muscles outside of the voice. We have an entire system of muscles dedicated to swallowing and controlling our head movements. If the body senses our voice is not up to the current task, it will start to employ these outer muscles. While the body may be well-intentioned, these muscles can cause excessive tension that creates a host of issues.

We want the vocal folds in an optimal state for phonation, giving us all the sound we need without extra effort. When we employ too much muscle to "help" the folds we end up putting too much strain and pressure on them. Excessive banging together of the folds can lead to chronic vocal issues.

The fine muscle coordination required for effective speaking is enhanced and reawakened during the warm-up phase.

Vocal warm-ups can help to clear away any excess mucus that may be coating the vocal folds. This will improve the clarity of the sound as well as ease of production.

A good vocal warm-up also has mental benefits, helping prepare you mentally for the upcoming talk. It can also help increase focus and confidence.

These warm-ups are effective, but they are not miracle workers. You need to do your part in taking care of your voice. As previously mentioned, ensure you get adequate sleep and hydration and avoid abuse from smoking or alcohol, especially the night before a big vocal day.

Start with taking your noble posture and inhaling deeply. Exhale with a controlled hiss. Feel the engagement of your stomach muscles as your ribs and chest maintain an outward and open posture.

Make an enthusiastic humming sound, "mmm hmmm." Feel the vibrations in your body and head. Move this hum up and down in pitch.

Slide from your lowest note to your highest on AH-OO. Then glide down from your high note to your low on OO-AH. Do this a few times, increasing the range.

Find your OSP with our enthusiastic humming sound, "mmm hmm." Feel the pitch inflect upwards. From this pitch, proclaim, "yes that's right!" And "absolutely!"

You can repeat these steps, especially the glides from lower to higher pitches as needed.

STRAW PHONATION

I want to give you what voice scientists believe is the best way to get your voice primed and ready quickly. It is phonating through a straw. By wrapping your lips around a drinking straw or a couple of cocktail straws and humming (much like playing the kazoo), you create optimal conditions for the voice to warm up.

I have artists on tour, playing for thousands of people, who keep vocalizing straws with them backstage. Before they step out, they go through the routine below.

I worked with a singer from a famous pop duo who was so impressed by the results of straw phonation that he showed his singing partner how to do it. It's simple and effective.

The straw essentially lengthens and narrows your vocal tract, creating a back pressure of air and sound wave energy. This back pressure acts like a mini massage, soothing your vocal folds and providing a cushion of air as they come together.

You will want to feel a certain amount of resistance when phonating through the straw. Allow your cheeks to puff out and a "bullfrog" sensation of expansion in the throat. If you don't feel this, try moving to a thinner straw. If you are using a drinking straw, try a couple of cocktail straws simultaneously.

Conversely, if phonation is a bit of a struggle, if you feel too much resistance, move to a bigger straw or add another cocktail straw. We want the resistance to be beneficial and balanced.

You can purchase reusable metal straws designed specifically for voice use. A search for "voice straw" will give you good choices.

EXERCISES:

While using the straw, glide up and down in pitch. Go slowly from your lowest to highest pitches.

Make a pulsing sound going from softer to louder. It can help to imitate a car engine trying to start.

Finally, do a short song like "Happy Birthday."

Remove the straw and say, "hello, how are you?" Does the voice feel different? It should feel lighter and easier to produce. You will likely be closer to your OSP as well.

When used properly, straws can give noticeable relief to tired voices. If I have a long vocal day, I will use a straw between sessions. Even seconds can make a difference.

I have created a video to walk you through the steps of using a straw in the members' area.

THE OLDER VOICE

"John, you have a benign essential vocal tremor."

The moment will never leave me. I had a slight sense of relief as I finally had an answer for my voice issues, but I was also overwhelmed by a sense of loss.

Until about a year before my diagnosis, my voice was always there for me, but in recent months it felt weak and not under my control, with flutters and spasms in my speaking voice that worsened when I tried to sing.

A vocal tremor is a misfiring of the nerves to the muscles of the voice, creating a quavering sound, making the speaker sound weak and prematurely old. Medical science is unsure of the cause, and there is no known cure.

I allowed myself a few minutes to grieve, and then I thanked the vocal gods for my new challenge. I was determined to regain my voice.

Rather than rely on current medical interventions, such as shots of Botox into the folds, I became focused on rebuilding my voice.

I turned to a fantastic speech-language pathologist and voice teacher, Kerrie Obert, who patiently and painstakingly worked my voice with a number of exercises.

These vocal workouts literally rewired my voice and strengthened the surrounding vocal tract to give me an anchor, which brought the tremors down to near zero.

I continue to work to keep my voice tremor free, and I am indeed thankful for the additional insight my struggle has given me for my clients.

The onset of this tremor also put into sharp relief the changes that can happen to my voice as I get older and my ability to delay or reduce these changes.

Aging is a complex process that affects all of us differently. Parts of our body can age more quickly than others. The voice is no exception; changes can be noticed as soon as one's 30s.

As with the body and overall health, taking care of the voice can extend your vocal prime and slow the aging process.

Here are some typical age-related voice issues that can occur.

Vocal Cord Atrophy: As we age, our vocal folds can become thinner and lose muscle bulk. This can lead to a breathy or weak voice.

Vocal Cord Bowing: Aging can lead to bowing or sagging of the vocal folds due to muscle weakness or atrophy. This can lead to a gap between the vocal folds when they should be closed, resulting in a hoarse or breathy voice.

Reduced Lung Capacity: Aging can lead to a reduction in lung capacity and breath control, which are both essential for strong, sustained vocal output. This can result in a quieter voice or reduced endurance while speaking.

Changes in Resonance: Age-related changes can also occur in the throat and oral cavity, affecting the resonance and quality of the voice. My tremor issue was helped by working exercises to re-strengthen the muscles of my vocal tract, resulting in improved resonance and power.

Decreased Saliva Production: Aging can also lead to decreased saliva production, which can cause a dry mouth and throat, impacting the voice quality. Thick mucus on the folds is often a result of this.

Health Conditions: Certain health conditions more common in older adults, like Parkinson's disease, stroke, or arthritis affecting the neck, can also affect the voice.

Changes in Pitch: The pitch of the voice can change with age, typically becoming higher in men (due to atrophy of the vocal folds) and lower in women (due to hormonal changes after menopause).

While extensive vocal rehab is beyond the scope of this book, I want you to be aware of these issues and to know there is help available. Do not hesitate to seek out a medical professional if you suspect any of these issues are occurring in your voice. An ENT can help diagnose and also refer a speech-language pathologist (SLP) for therapeutic exercises.

CHAPTER TWELVE

Vocal Confidence

"Inaction breeds doubt and fear. Action breeds confidence and courage. If you want to conquer fear, do not sit home and think about it. Go out and get busy."

– DALE CARNEGIE

Confidence is a mysterious force; it can feel somewhat elusive and often out of our control. It's a quality that's both how we perceive ourselves as well as how we're perceived by others. The listener will use their personal criteria to decide whether I am confident, trustworthy, and what level of authority I might hold.

But of course, the less confident you feel, the less likely the other party will see you in a positive light.

You can't fake real confidence when there's no good reason to be sure of yourself. Knowledge is paramount. If I walk before a group to discuss the voice, I am confident of my knowledge and abilities, but if I were to lecture on improving your tennis game, I would panic.

But even knowledgeable people can have their confidence wane in higher-pressure situations, especially in public speaking and presenting.

This is why I am so passionate about building your speaking skills. Knowing your voice sounds great and using it in a wonderfully musical way can make public speaking less terrifying and even fun! And if you are having fun, you will appear incredibly confident.

We all know what it's like to be easily and naturally confident. The comfort and security of being around loved ones, the ease of conversation, and knowing what you are saying is being welcomed and listened to.

Those wonderful small wins in life, when we complete a project, or exercise when we didn't feel like it. Pay attention to your sense of self in those moments. This is what natural confidence feels like.

However, there are a few ways we can self-sabotage our inner confidence; they include allowing impostor syndrome to take root, negative self-talk, or not being prepared.

Being prepared and consistently increasing your knowledge is essential. This book is not about faking your way through, and if you have made it this far, you are diligent and knowledgeable.

But even the most knowledgeable and prepared speaker can experience doubt and loss of confidence. Let's discuss a few of the main issues.

IMPOSTOR SYNDROME

Impostor syndrome is a form of distorted self-perception that I find somewhat common in thought leaders and entrepreneurs.

Persistent and pervasive impostor syndrome can be a debilitating issue. If you are experiencing distress, you might want to seek the help of a mental health professional.

Not all bouts of impostor syndrome are severe, yet they can stop us from attaining our goals.

Conscientious people are ever questioning their skills and knowledge, and a certain amount of this is healthy and necessary.

A small sprinkling of impostor syndrome can lead to humility, empathy, drive, and continual learning. It is when we allow those doubts and comparisons to others to overwhelm us that impostor syndrome becomes a genuine problem.

I experience impostor syndrome from time to time, especially when I am faced with a large project that will be viewed by peers and incredibly smart people.

I am also on guard for its imminent arrival and have a few safeguards in place that I would like to share with you in the hopes they will help when the self-critical monster is at your door.

First, I stop comparing myself to others. I'm not saying never to compare as we should keep up with our profession, but when facing impostor syndrome, I know comparisons are likely not mentally healthy and will no doubt be framed in the negative.

We are all unique in our backgrounds, skill sets, and how we communicate and instruct.

Very few singers can sing like Beyoncé and they don't need to. Some of my favorite artists are not perfect singers but bring uniqueness to their art. This is why they are compelling.

I know there are a great deal of books that cover speaking, and fantastic experts have written them. But I also know I will connect with some of you differently and that I may be the one who helps you achieve a breakthrough.

There are people who not only need to hear what you know, but they need to hear it from you. Giving in and indulging the negative self-talk and emotions of impostor syndrome potentially robs them of your unique gifts and knowledge.

I bring up impostor syndrome because it is often an accomplice of a greater fear and inhibitor of spreading your skills and knowledge... stage fright!

STAGE FRIGHT

"According to most studies, people's number one fear is public speaking. Number two is death. Death is number two. Does that sound right? This means to the average person if you go to a funeral, you're better off in the casket than doing the eulogy."
– Jerry Seinfeld

Glossophobia, also known as speech anxiety, is the fear of public speaking. It's a very common form of anxiety ranging from slight nervousness to paralyzing fear and panic. Many people with this fear avoid public speaking situations altogether, or if they must speak in public, they suffer significant anxiety symptoms.

Stage fright plays a complex role in performance. When stage fright becomes severe, it can impede the performer's ability to concentrate, leading to mistakes, forgetfulness, and decreased performance quality.

However, a moderate amount of anxiety or nervousness can actually enhance performance. This concept is known as the Yerkes-Dodson law, which proposes that performance improves with physiological or mental arousal (stress) but only up to a point. When levels of arousal become too high, performance decreases. A certain level of stress can heighten awareness, increase energy, and keep performers "on their toes," leading to a better performance.

When I am about to go onstage or begin an online lecture, I certainly experience Yerkes-Dodson. While I welcome this heightened state, I know this state is tenuous and can easily tip over into stage fright.

Here is what I do in these situations:

First, I realize this fear is primal and not rooted in my present reality.

Stage fright is related to primal fears and the wiring of the brain. It has roots in the "fight or flight" response, a basic survival mechanism that originated in our prehistoric ancestors.

When faced with a threat, the brain releases adrenaline, causing increased heart rate, blood pressure, and blood sugar levels to prepare the body for immediate action. In the case of stage fright, the "threat" is the prospect of performing in front of an audience and potentially making a mistake or being judged negatively. Even though this isn't a physical threat, the brain can still react as if it is.

Some psychologists believe the fear of public speaking or performance (which leads to stage fright) might be related to ancient fears of being ostracized from the group. In prehistoric times, being rejected or expelled could mean loss of protection, resources, and ultimately survival. Therefore, individuals who were accepted by their group were more likely to survive and reproduce.

It makes sense we have a deeply ingrained fear of doing anything that could lead to social rejection, such as embarrassing ourselves in public. When in front of an audience, the risk of embarrassment and subsequent social rejection feels high, which could trigger a strong anxiety response, leading to stage fright.

The fear is visceral, yet there is no danger except to the ego. By turning inward (ego), my state turns from healthy nervousness and anticipation to creeping fear. When I feel this, I have a few pattern interrupts that work exceptionally well for me.

Note: serious stage fright can require the help of a mental health professional.

When confronted with rising anxiety, I immediately stop and remind myself that it is not about me. People have taken time out of their day (voluntarily or not), and what I have to tell them is more important than what I feel.

I focus on all the corners of the room I will speak in and think of filling the space with my energy, sending the sense of self outward. If I feel a contraction into myself, the negative self-talk, I once again say, "it's not about me."

I then do something I learned long ago. I give the audience permission not to like me. They have the right to reject you and what you are saying, and you will never reach everyone.

"You do not have to like me. I accept this and grant you this permission. However, I am here for those who want or need to hear what I have to say. I will focus my energy and attention on them."

The sense of self is powerful but also a bit of an illusion. Meditation is an effective way to experience this "self" in different ways and reverse the inward turn and the shackles of thought in these circumstances. When you can be open, present, and outward-focused, stage fright tends to fall away to a positive, manageable state of readiness.

THE WAY THROUGH

"The best way out is always through."
– Robert Frost

I am reminded of this quote whenever someone asks how to overcome anxiety when speaking or singing. The way around this problem is to go through it.

We should be forgiving of ourselves when trying a new skill, especially in front of others. There will be a natural degradation of our skill set at first, so it might be best to move up gradually.

I made this mistake when I was first learning to sing. At the time, I was doing regular performances as a drummer and had yet to tell people I was studying voice. One night, on a whim, I asked if I could take the lead on a song, one with a high degree of difficulty. The band leader looked surprised but agreed, likely due to curiosity. Since the song was a ballad with no drums, I stood at the front of the stage with no drum set to hide behind.

As I started to sing, my voice coming from the monitors back at me was jarring, another unfamiliarity. I could feel the panic build up, and then...my voice cracked.

In my peripheral vision, I saw the bass player and guitarist look at each other and start laughing. Side note: musicians love to bust each other for wrong notes and mistakes.

At that moment, I would have been so happy to have the earth swallow me whole, to make the next three minutes disappear. I don't remember getting through the song, but it would be a while before I tried again.

My mistake was jumping too far forward in my attempt to "go through." I have seen this with clients; they are put in a situation far above their prior experience. This can throw off a natural progression.

The important part of my story was I did continue to perform but on a better trajectory. I started doing backup vocals and taking leads on easier songs. By reducing the difficulty level and allowing a more gradual progression, I could once again stand at the front of the stage and tackle the more challenging material.

Speaking in front of others is a skill, and the more you do it, the better you will get.

Start by practicing alone. I recommend using a mirror at times, but don't become obsessed with staring at yourself. You don't want to practice turning inward and being self-focused. Again, the key to compelling speaking is to become focused on the listener.

Music is a great parallel. When young or less experienced musicians play together, their focus and attention tend to be on themselves and what they are playing or singing. As they gain experience, their focus shifts outward to the other musicians and the performance as a whole. They will direct less and less attention at themselves until their playing becomes one with the whole.

So it is with speaking. The more you speak and communicate in these situations, the more you are focused on the content and the listener. There is a beautiful vanishing of the self.

Then give shortened versions of your talk for friends and loved ones. Accept constructive criticism, but don't make it personal.

Allow criticism to make you better. The truth is, the more you speak, the more you will be heard, and the more criticisms may come your way. This will be a part of your rising influence.

You should then start seeking out speaking opportunities. Volunteer to lead meetings or presentations. Continue to build your speaking muscle.

After a presentation, do a review. Ask yourself:

How did that feel?

Was I able to stay focused on the listeners and material?

What intentions could have been used to better effect?

Was my voice feeling strong and confident?

Use your answers to find areas to work on. Constant small improvements will accumulate and provide momentum. As you build skills and confidence, speaking in front of others will become enjoyable rather than a source of fear.

It is invigorating to enter the flow of performance and lose yourself in the energy of an inspired presentation. The way round is indeed through.

CHAPTER THIRTEEN

Taking the Stage

"It's all right to have butterflies in your stomach.
Just get them to fly in formation."
– ROB GILBERT

Now comes showtime. For a singer, it's when all the hours in the practice room (and all the previous performances) pay off. This is an exciting and powerful moment! You are building a skill set that will have profound and lasting effects on your life and career.

Let's discuss how to make the most of these opportunities.

I must once again emphasize how crucial it is to be prepared. No matter how good I can make my voice sound, I cannot be effective without proper preparation.

Know your material well enough to talk about it freely without any slides. You should also be able to answer most reasonable questions.

As a working musician, there are times when you have to learn a song at the last minute, trying to hide lyrics onstage to get through the song. Although I had enough experience to "fake it," these rarely resulted in my best performances.

By preparing your material and the command of your voice, you will be well-placed to lead a compelling talk.

OWNING THE STAGE

The moments just before taking the stage are crucial. You want to spend them getting your mindset focused and ready. I recommend having a routine so your mind doesn't wander and find reasons to panic.

Many famous performers have rituals they engage in before taking the stage. Meditation or finding a quiet moment to focus is a common one. Luciano Pavarotti would always find a nail (from the opera set construction) and place it in his pocket as a good luck ritual.

I go through my own steps just before taking the stage.

First, I stand off to myself and close my eyes, focusing on my breath. I then remind myself I am not here for me but for those who have come to listen. I then give permission for listeners not to like me.

I then shift my focus outward and mentally expand my energy and focus to all the corners of the room. Performers possess a keen sense of their physical environment and their own energy within it. This external redirection can significantly impact how one engages with the audience.

Lastly, I remind myself of my emotional intention, my goal for the event. I am now ready to step on stage.

When you step out, don't rush. Allow yourself to take in the audience and greet them warmly and sincerely.

Feel your energy and presence fill the room and include everyone in it. The key word is "outward"; everything is focused on the audience. If the inner chatter begins, remind yourself to FOCUS OUT, not in.

EYE CONTACT

Eye contact is important but don't overdo it. Quick glances of recognition and connection are a great way to keep your energy flowing with the audience, but eye contact that goes too long quickly becomes uncomfortable.

An effective trick I use is to imagine a movie playing on the back wall, just above the audience's head. The images I see are aligned with my intention at that moment. If my intention is "to inspire," then I see people enthusiastically cheering. If my intention is "to instruct" I see people deep in learning. The movie can be anything. If my intention is "to celebrate," I see a beautiful sunrise and even puppies.

When you imagine this movie, your eyes and focus concentrate, and you appear fully attentive and present.

Now move the movie to different parts of the wall. Start in the center and then move it to the left or right. These moves will project your visual energy to other parts of the room.

As I make certain points, I might bring my eyes back to the audience, making quick eye contact with one individual or section, then at the audience as a whole, and then back to the movie on the back wall.

There is, as in all things, a balance. Allow this to flow rather than quickly darting around. By keeping a shifting focus of visual energy, you allow the audience to observe and watch you, briefly personally connect, and then go back to being the observer. It is a powerful way to establish rapport.

BODY LANGUAGE

Quite a bit is made about body language, and while it is important, I don't want you to feel stiff or overthink it.

There are a few concepts that will go a long way—first, your posture. You will likely be in a tall, noble stance if you have been doing the breathing exercises. It's not a sway back or a stiff ramrod holding of the body. Allow yourself to be flowing and walk like a great athlete taking the field.

Your hands and arms, what to do with them? When I was first standing in front of the stage, I felt lost with my hands. I was used to having drumsticks to keep them busy.

It is odd to be in front of others and suddenly feel like we don't know what to do with our arms and hands. Some speakers will clasp them together or hold them stiffly at their sides. But your hands are incredibly expressive and part of your communication.

I struggled with this until a brilliant acting coach, Carole D'Andrea, told me "just leave them alone." She pointed out that I don't worry about my hands when having a lively discussion with friends. Allow your arms and hands to be a natural part of the communication process without forcing them.

This applies to facial expressions as well. When you allow your emotional intentions to take the driver's seat, everything will naturally follow. It may take a few tries before this feels natural, but the more natural you are, the more compelling.

MOVEMENT

The center stage is akin to your OSP. It is the "center," but you don't want to be stuck there. Moving on stage is essential, but it shouldn't appear nervous or haphazard.

A good rule is to start moving on a new point or intention. This makes the energy of the move feel deliberate and driven by the material. The speed and length of the move is also driven by emotional content. If you are making a quiet, more serious point, your movement would be less than during a passionate, emotional peak.

Another rule to be aware of is moving toward the audience (downstage) or backing away (upstage). Be careful about moving upstage as it tends to project weakness, while moving downstage shows power.

SWAYING

When you stand in one spot, ensure your stance is planted and your body energy is rooted down to your feet. Again, while you don't want to be rigid, you also don't want to fall into a nervous swaying. This sway comes off as nervousness or restlessness rather than natural movement or physical expression.

THE AUDIENCE

Audiences can be fickle, with focused attention ebbing and flowing. While you cannot hold everyone's attention at all times, there will be moments when you feel the energy and focus start to slip. People will rustle in their chairs and begin to look around. This is where pattern interrupts are a valuable resource.

Singers know the repetitive nature of songs requires something extra to keep movement and interest. Your musical voice will serve the same purpose. Think of a DJ drop, the building of intensity with a sudden pullback or break, only to build the music up again.

The "drop" is a dramatic pattern interrupt, and it is very effective. When you feel the audience slip away, use a pattern interrupt. A quick rise in volume, with a sudden pause, will grab even the most distracted listener. Moving from information to a brief, relevant story can have the same effect.

STORYTELLING

The effectiveness of storytelling is often celebrated, and rightly so, as a great story or even quick metaphor can make an impact in ways that straight information can't. But be careful and sparing with your stories. Make them count.

I remember attending a two-day conference for music educators. There was only one speaker for both eight-hour days, a daunting task.

As we began the first day's session, he told a slightly amusing anecdote to get things going before delving into the first of his slides. Soon, however, I watched the time drag on as shorter anecdotes were replaced by longer stories and rambling jokes. I realized our two days could have been easily compressed into one. A definite example of overuse.

We have all been around excellent storytellers who can light up a room with humor and wit. We have also endured the non-stop talker whose stories go nowhere and have little to do with what is being discussed.

Storytelling involves several key elements that can captivate and engage your audience. Here are some tips to help you craft and deliver a compelling story:

Choose a relevant and relatable topic: Select a story that aligns with your talk's theme or purpose. Ensure it resonates with your audience and relates to their experiences or interests.

Establish a clear structure: Organize your story into a clear beginning, middle, and end. Introduce the main characters, set the scene, develop the plot, and provide a resolution or key takeaway.

Create a compelling opening: Grab your audience's attention from the start. Begin with a hook, an intriguing question, or a captivating statement that immediately captures their interest.

Develop vivid descriptions: Use descriptive language to paint a picture and engage your audience's senses. Help them visualize the setting, characters, and emotions involved in the story.

Show, don't just tell: Instead of simply stating facts or events, bring your story to life by incorporating dialogue, actions, and emotions. Let your audience experience the story alongside you.

Use pacing and timing: Vary your pace and tone to match the mood of the story. Slow down during emotional or impactful moments and speed up during action-packed or exciting parts.

Inject humor or emotion: Depending on the nature of your story, incorporate appropriate humor or emotional elements. This can help to connect with your audience on a deeper level and make your story more memorable.

Tie it to a broader message: Ensure that your story has a purpose and aligns with the main message or lesson you want to convey. Connect the story to the broader context of your speech to make it relevant and meaningful.

Practice and refine: Rehearse your story multiple times to become comfortable with its delivery. Pay attention to your body language, facial expressions, and vocal delivery to enhance the overall impact.

While speaking on stage or in front of a large group can be an exhilarating experience, there is another stage where you will likely spend more time, the online meeting.

VIRTUAL MEETINGS AND VIDEO

I was working with a top voiceover artist, someone you have undoubtedly heard if you live in the USA as her voice is featured in major advertising campaigns. I asked her the secret to a great voiceover.

She answered with a question; "How many people do you think I am talking to when I read an ad?"

"I don't know, millions?"

"One," she replied. "I am only speaking to one person."

This was a profound lesson about focus and connection, relevant to all forms of communication, but particularly applicable to meetings and videos. This experienced professional understood that by channeling her energy and intention towards "one person," she could amplify her message and make it resonate personally with every individual listener.

Virtual meetings are now commonplace as the workplace has undergone huge changes. Remote work and the convenience of virtually meeting face-to-face have replaced a portion of business travel with its expense and inconvenience.

But virtual meetings are where many lose their charisma and energy. The camera and a computer screen lack the interaction and immediacy of being in the room.

This can cause virtual meetings to be lackluster and somewhat unpleasant to sit through.

However, there is an opportunity to create energy and capture attention, to make yourself heard. What works when standing in front of a group of people works virtually as well. Musicians and actors have been dealing with this for 100 years. The move from the stage to the recording studio or movie set requires a shift that retains the energy of the live setting. A vocal performance in the studio is not the same as live, but there is no drop in energy.

The biggest mistake I see is sitting in your office alone with the camera and engaging as if people are miles away. The camera is a tool that you will look towards (sort of) and speak into while staring at the screen with the digital images of your fellow attendees.

I recommend making the camera (and your whole room) the focus of your energy. Just as in a live situation, allow your presence to fill your space and make the camera the center of it. Including the camera as an actual being, someone you are enveloping in your energy will transmit across the digital realm. Stare right into the camera with your energy and emotional intentions.

Your musical voice is essential as there are more distractions on the other side of the screen. By treating the virtual meeting with the same focus as a live one, you will be instantly more compelling, and you will have a much better chance of interacting and communicating on a deeper level.

ADJUSTING FOR SITUATIONS

The tips and lessons in this book are to be used situationally, never as rigid rules. There will be times when you don't need to engage these tools, such as quick exchanges, asking for information, etc. But in important moments, where what you have to say or your ability to convince has larger stakes, you now have an extra edge.

The key to communication is not only in talking; it is in listening as well. Become a keen observer of others. The more you need to be heard, the more you need to listen.

One of the best compliments you can give a musician is to tell them they have great ears, an ability to hear and listen to what is happening around them. The better the musician, the more they are focused on others.

Keep your focus outward and respond in real-time to what you are hearing. Use your voice for the music in the moment. Remember, the human voice is THE carrier and communicator of emotion and intention on a deeper level than the words being spoken. We already have the ability to intuit and discern, if we only listen.

CHAPTER FOURTEEN

Next Steps and Resources

"Learning never exhausts the mind."
– LEONARDO DA VINCI

I hope you have a new awareness and appreciation for your voice, as well as other great voices. I encourage you to seek out and listen to inspiring speakers. As I listen to fantastic communicators, I pay attention to the whole of their energy and connection, as well as the nuances.

Listen to their pitch and range and how they shift tone and intensity. How do they utilize tempo and rhythm? When they reach an important point, what do they do musically with the voice? What is the build and payoff?

The clues are there. Just as singers pore over and analyze their favorite vocal performances, you can learn so much from effective communicators. The goal is not to imitate but to reinforce what you now know and to see and hear communication in a new way.

I also encourage you to come back to these exercises, more frequently at first, to establish the vocal habits, and then on a somewhat regular basis to keep your voice tuned and ready to engage with others.

As you practice, these new elements will start finding their way into your voice and everyday communication. And then, when the communication stakes are raised, you can dial up the music and intentions to meet the moment.

What may seem stiff and forced at first will give way to a natural rhythm and flow. By continuing to work on your new skills and awareness, you will be able to use your voice like the beautiful instrument it is, able to adapt and adjust to any situation with appropriate tone and intention.

If you would like help, I have online courses and one-on-one sessions available with me and my team.

Reach out to frontdesk@compellingspeaker.com, and we would be honored to help you reach new levels of communication and influence.

I would also love to hear how these techniques have helped you. Please feel free to reach out to me at john@compellingspeaker.com.

I wish you much success and music. Remember, every time you form words, you are singing, as our ancestors did all those years ago. And this music can't help but bring your ideas and passion to others on a deeper level. You are the song, your voice is the music, and we all need to hear you.

Here are a few resources to help you in your vocal journey.

Dr. Reena Gupta
Dr. Gupta is a top laryngologist in Los Angeles who maintains a blog of voice articles focused on health.
https://www.centerforvocalhealth.com/blog

Dr. Steven Sims
Dr. Sims is based in Chicago and offers telehealth consultations. https://www.chicagovoicecare.com/

NCVS
The National Center for Voice and Speech is a leading voice science research facility. They have a comprehensive guide to prescription medications and the possible effects on the voice.
https://ncvs.org/prescriptions/

Voice Straw
These voice straws were designed in conjunction with the creator of straw phonation, Dr. Ingo Titze. The straws are the right length and diameter for maximum results.
https://voicestraw.com/

Actions: The Actors' Thesarus by Marina Caldarone and Maggie Lloyd-Williams
This book is a fantastic reference for finding emotional intentions.

Compelling Speaker
My website featuring blogs and helpful information for professional voice users. You can also find out more about my online course and working with me directly.
https://www.compellingspeaker.com/

John Henny

This is my main website for all things singing. If I have piqued your interest in developing your voice in this area, you can find blog articles and my podcast, The Intelligent Vocalist.

https://johnhenny.com/

What Did You Think?

As the author of 'The Compelling Speaker', I am genuinely interested in your thoughts about the book. Your feedback not only helps me improve future works, but it also aids fellow readers in their choice of reading material.

If you found value in this book or have any insights to share, please leave a review on Amazon. Your review will make a tremendous difference and is deeply appreciated.

To leave a review, just head over to the Amazon page where you purchased 'The Compelling Speaker' and click on 'Write a customer review'.

Thank you in advance for your time and your thoughtful feedback.

About the Author

John Henny has decades of experience helping thousands of voice users around the world become more effective communicators.

He is a featured lecturer at top voice conferences and institutions, including IVTOM, Osborne Head and Neck Institute, VIP Worldwide Voice Conference, The Paul McCartney Liverpool Institute and USC.

John is the author of three Amazon bestselling books, hosts the popular podcast The Intelligent Vocalist and his YouTube channel has well over 100,000 subscribers.

Also by John Henny

Beginning Singing: Expand Your Range, Improve Your Tone, and Create a Voice You'll Love

Teaching Contemporary Singing: The Proven Method for Becoming a Successful, Confident Voice Teacher and Getting Vocal Breakthroughs for Your Students

Voice Teacher Influencer: Grow Your Studio, Increase Your Authority, and Make More Money

www.ingramcontent.com/pod-product-compliance
Lightning Source LLC
Chambersburg PA
CBHW072147090426
42739CB00013B/3307